A COMPILATION OF STORIES OF VICTORY

OUR STORIES
His Glory

SPEAKLIFE SERIES

A COMPILATION OF STORIES OF VICTORY

SPEAKLIFE SERIES

Scripture quotations are taken from the Holy Bible, New Living Translation (NIV), copyright © 1996, 2004, 2007, 2013, 2015 by Tyndale House Foundation.

Editing: SynergyEd Consulting/ synergyedconsulting.com
Graphics & Cover Design: Greenlight Creations Graphics Designs
glightcreations.com/ glightcreations@gmail.com

shero
publishing

Published by: SHERO Publishing
getpublished@sheropublishing.com
S H E R O P U B L I S H I N G . C O M

Be it advised that all information within this literary work, OUR STORIES HIS GLORY, has been acknowledged to be the truthful account of each co-author. The authors are responsible for the content in their individual chapter and hold SHERO Publishing harmless for any legal action arising as a result of their participation in this publication.

L A T I C I A N I C O L E . C O M

SPEAKLIFE SERIES

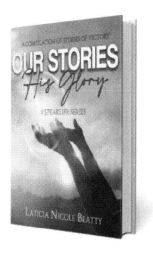

A COMPILATION OF STORIES OF VICTORY

A COMPILATION OF STORIES OF VICTORY

SPEAKLIFE SERIES

Table of Contents

Stories of Victory

Acknowledgments

I want to send a special thank you to everyone who believed in me and in the value of this book. That list includes (but is certainly not limited to):

My Mother Nora Pitts and Father Gregory Stanton
My Husband Antonio Beatty and two boys; Antonio & Aden Beatty
My Pastor Rose Thomas
Erica Perry Green and the SHERO Publishing Team
Pamela Mitchell
Kimberly Taylor
Kimberly Guess
Jewell Tillman
Tanisha Coleman
Michael Green
Juanita Brunson
Eraina Tinnin
Lenita Henderson
Laurine Garner
Melanie Smiles
Samantha Williams
Samantha Huntley
Sean Bethea
Monique Chantel Johnson
Alicia Spivey Johnson
Jermain Smith
Sharon Dye
Toy Nicole
Pam Thompson Smith
Amy Timmons Miles
Umeka Jackson
Tonya Miller Cross

Introduction

God has been telling me to write this story for a couple years now. I was moved to facilitate a conference, on a cruise first, however, back in November 2019. I had about 30 women who went on that cruise with me, and I had about seven speakers. Each one of us had a testimony. One of the ladies shared a testimony about her husband who had been abusive and unfaithful.

After listening to the testimony, you could hear this voice say, "I have something to say." We all looked around, wondering who said it. Turns out, it was a 71-year-old woman who quote, unquote was not even supposed to be there. I intentionally quoted and unquoted her presence because they were her words for one, and for two, I do not believe in accidents nor in coincidence. For better or worse, it is all divinely orchestrated.

So, although she nor her family knew anything about the conference, they were there. They all bought t-shirts, wore them, and blended in with everyone else in attendance. They were also positioned in the right place, at the right time, to hear the right testimony to move this 71-year-old woman to tell her story.

"I didn't want to be on this cruise, but God had a plan," she said, "I wanted to kill myself. I wanted to die. My husband of 50 years left me, my grandchildren, my great-grandchildren for another woman. My husband of 50 years. Why did he do this to me?"

She said she wanted to take her life, so her children and grandchildren took her on a cruise that she really did not want to be on. But she was glad that she did. "I...am...free!" she added.

The whole room was in tears, and I ended up presenting to her a trophy of triumph which was originally awarded to me two years before. She was supposed to be there, as we all were. Her being inspired to tell her story reminded me once again why it was so important for me to write this book.

Revelations 12:11 (NIV) says, *They triumphed over him by the blood of the Lamb and by the word of their testimony; they did not love their lives so much as to shrink from death.* They triumphed over the enemy. They won. They beat him, and by the word of their testimony—meaning our word, our testimony, the stuff we went through.

We overcome by the blood of the lamb and by the words of our testimony, that we will not shrink our own life to other people. We tell what happened, because it is nobody's business to dictate what parts of our stories we can tell and which we can not. We are not ashamed of our stories and we give God glory because we made it to the other side.

I wrote this book to gather the testimonies of how 16 people, including myself, broke out of bondage to be free to tell it so other people can get free and stop being under bondage of other people. Too many of us are afraid to say what really happened, how many abortions they had, how many times they've been in failed relationships, abusive relationships, how many times they've been talked about, how many times they've been molested, that they were down and out.

Our stories are the bridge from the side of feeling shame and isolation to being free and emboldened. But how are others supposed get to the other side unless we tell what happened (and even what is happening—present tense) to us?

I plan to continue this series until God tells me to stop, because this vision is bigger than me. I have learned that when God gives you a vision, He gives it to you for other people. Your job is to get out of their way. That is why **Our Stories, His Glory** was birthed—to give you the stories, the bridge, to open yourself to His will so that you can get out of the way. After all, people are waiting for you to build their bridge.

It is time to peel that layers of the onion. It is a process. After you read this book, decide which story relates to you. Read all of them to find yourself or your sister or your brother, so you can have empathy and not be so quick to judge. Disregard those who ask, "Why are you telling all your business?" You might be on day 50 or day 10,000 of your class on forgiveness and healing, whereas they are only on day 2. Give them grace because they do not understand the healing process yet. They do not understand that you do not care who knows what you have been through. You are not afraid anymore. The enemy has gotten way too much glory and you have been in way too much pain. Let go.

The book cover shows hands lifted to God towards the sun, because whom the sun sets free is free indeed. The hands signify giving God glory for that story, and the words are written in red to symbolize the blood of the lamb. We have already been redeemed. We have already been paid for with a price. God knew we would go through everything we went through and come out alive with our faith stretched and strengthened.

But you must be willing to let go, and the stories herein will show you just how to.

OUR STORIES
His Glory

SPEAKLIFE SERIES

A COMPILATION OF STORIES OF VICTORY

Author Alicia Spivey Johnson

Author Alicia Spivey Johnson

Alicia Spivey Johnson is a wife, mother and self-proclaimed *Serial Entrepreneur*. Alicia was born in New York and raised in North Carolina. Upon graduation from King College in Charlotte, NC, Alicia moved to Raleigh-Durham, a place that would prove to be a great catalyst for her entrepreneurial spirit. Alicia was self-aware of her outgoing and tenacious personality and decided to use those qualities to pursue a career in sales. Ambitious and eager to accomplish more, Alicia went on to obtain her real estate license.

Outside of real estate, Alicia wears many other hats. She is an author of her published book entitled *Don't Question Your Flow: Your Mission Motivates Your Money*. Alicia is a Financial Commercial Consultant with twenty-six years at Commercial Capital, where she is a Certified Personal and Business Credit Specialist. In the medical field, she is a Certified Medical Billing and Coding Specialist. If that's not enough, Alicia is also a motivational speaker and a Mobile Notary Signing Agent.

Alicia's goal-oriented, no-nonsense mentality is taking her even further. She is using her personal experiences as a multi-faceted business woman to help small business owners secure their company's financial stability by teaching them about business credit and assisting them in getting funds. Alicia knows what it means to make goals, commit and achieve. She has successfully balanced being a wife, mother and entrepreneur and she now hopes to inspire others to balance their personal pursuits with their family and professional lives. Alicia believes that everyone can shine and achieve their greatest potential, and she wants to help.

Alicia has been in the trenches- where you find yourself at this moment. She is now following her calling to help others find their paths in a complicated world, because when no one was around, she found her way and rewrote her story.

Alicia is committed to collaborating with her clients to assist them in leading "a life beyond limits." Her approach is compassionate, curious, and resilient. Her goal is to empower her clients to embody their own best selves, every day.

Alicia is heavily engaged with community involvement in the following areas:

- Certified Success Coach
- Member of Iota Phi Lambda Sorority
- Real Estate Professional
- Commercial Loan Broker

Having lived and learned through the vicissitudes of starting a mission-driven company, Alicia is passionate about supporting others who want to contribute their talents toward a calling that fully inspires them.

Connect with Alicia Spivey Johnson:
Facebook: fb.me/26realtygroup
LinkedIn: linkedin.com/in/alicia-spivey-johnson-59827a30

Resilience- Never Give Up!

W hat does *resilience* mean to me? It's knowing how to cope in spite of setbacks, barriers or limited resources. It has a lot to do with your emotional strength. I express my gratitude to the many people who saw my changes and still supported my visions.

Growing up as a country girl, my self-esteem was very low. I grew up thinking I was weak, unattractive and lacked a vision. It took many years of self-development to get to a place where I learned to love myself.

There is power in the universe. I began to meditate. I have always created vision boards. However, during my season of intentional, focused growth – I started speaking and observing the *law of attraction.*

Are you familiar with the *law of attraction*? Simply explained, it is the belief that -you attract into your life anything you give attention to, regardless if it is positive or negative. The *law of attraction* is constantly working to deliver to you what you constantly think about on a business or personal level.

In 2010, I was at one of my lowest points. I cried almost every day. My career was on the rocks, my family was falling apart and I felt helpless. I was always taught to pray about *it*. God will answer your prayers. Yes, I do believe in the power of prayer; and I did pray. However, to maintain my mental survival, I had to find a way to empower myself.

I decided to *design my life*! I recognized that setbacks and failures are going to happen. The question I had for myself was- *how will I overcome them?*

My Story...

My husband and I were considering divorce. For a number of years, I believed he was unfaithful; yet I continued to stay in an unhealthy relationship out of fear. I blamed myself for not being pretty enough. I blamed myself for not making the home happy. I convinced myself that these deficiencies were the reasons we were having marriage problems. At my tipping point, my husband lost his job, and we ended up losing some real estate assets due to the market crashing. Taking the higher ground, I again decided to continue to stay in the relationship, and not leave a man when he's down. At this point, I decided to invest in my vision of becoming an entrepreneur. I created vision boards and posted them throughout the house. It was also during this time that I started watching the series - "The Secret".

I blamed myself that our strong-willed daughter was rebellious against everyone, especially my husband and me. I believed that I wasn't a good role model. My daughter was beautiful and advanced beyond her age. Unfortunately, she had difficulty taking directions from her teachers and parents. She was determined things had to be done her way. She vocalized threats and was destroying property at home as a way of acting out. This affected everyone. It started when she was in the 8th grade. We tried everything as parents. Her unacceptable, disrespectful behavior resulted in her having to be moved out of the home when she was in 10th grade. In her senior year of high school, she returned to live at home. However, not much had changed with her lack of respect...so I decided to begin traveling more with my entrepreneurship.

I blamed myself for not having enough income because I didn't have a college degree. Let me assure you there is *power in resilience.* I knew I had to create a roadmap to change my situation. I started believing in myself and my talents. I started studying my craft; watching YouTube videos, and educating myself on real estate, personal credit, business credit, business funding, and consulting. As my knowledge and competence increased, I grew more confident. Using all that I learned, I created multiple businesses and ran with the endless opportunities that manifested.

I decided to try a spiritual healing called *Reiki*. *Reiki* is a spiritual healing that works by channeling positive energy into your body. The powerful flow of positive energy may bring a sensation of relief. Some refer to this positive *Reiki* energy as the new life force. This experience taught me how to get in touch with my mind, body and spirit. I meditated daily; seeking answers and asking for power. And the Holy Spirit delivered! I was about to obtain ALL my dreams; I paid my daughter's way through college, purchased fancy clothes and luxury cars such as a Porsche, Range Rover, Lexus, and Rolls Royce. And there was so much more! I went from losing my income and some of our real estate investment properties in 2010, to achieving multimillionaire status for several years!

"Every time you state what you want to believe, you're the first to hear it. It's a message to both you and others about what you think is possible. Don't put a ceiling on yourself" – Oprah Winfrey.

As entrepreneurs, none of our businesses succeed without the support of those around us: family, friends, partners, team members, suppliers, investors, and clients/customers. I can acknowledge that I put too much trust in some of my supporters, and my businesses took a hit when I made some poor business decisions.

YEP !

Setbacks and Failures. Then life happened again.

In 2017, another career shift affected my income. Yes, I lost millions! The business took a massive loss that resulted in massive stress, exorbitant legal fees, and financial pain. Fortunately, I still had other businesses that I could fall back upon as I began to rebuild and refocus. During this devastation of my businesses, my son, age 17 hit a challenging spot in his life. This caused him to be hospitalized four times within 30 days, but I knew the power of *resilience*. The doctors had limited answers. Although we all actually knew the source of my son's problems, we all were in denial.

I dropped everything to care for my son. We both continued to meditate but none of the problems went away. The business losses, legal fees, health issues, relationship problems; they all persisted. I wasn't sleeping or eating. I was totally overwhelmed.

Yes, I started praying.

Yes, I started taking a sleep aid.

Yes, I started receiving personal counseling

Yes, the challenges still existed.

We all will have *setbacks and failures,* but we can choose to make excuses or we can choose to be *resilient!*

TAKE ACTION!

Evaluate the failures and setbacks.
- What was it?
- How did it occur?
- Why did it happen?
- What's the solution?
- How can it be prevented in the future?

The hard work of writing this chapter was a healing process for me. I encourage you to continue to learn, grow and NEVER GIVE UP on your dreams

Never give up.... 23 years later – **yes, I am still married.** Each day my husband and I are actively working on our relationship. During the process of contemplating divorce; during the midst of overwhelming challenges, my husband and I decided that we were *partners*. We agreed that no matter what the challenges, we would work on our marriage and save our family! I want to thank everyone who prayed for us and continued to pray for us. It wasn't easy; a lot has changed for my husband and a lot has changed for me. We have agreed to keep God as the head, and we know that God will order our steps. I want to give a special thank you to my parents who ALWAYS lead by example.

NEVER GIVE UP

It's with great pleasure that I share that my Super-Star daughter has graduated from North Carolina A & T State University with a bachelor's degree in social work. She has also completed her master's degree in social work from the University of South Carolina. She is currently completing her doctorate in psychology from Walden University. Although I thought she wasn't listening or taking our advice, sometimes we don't know God's plan. I am so very, very proud of her and all her accomplishments. She is beautiful, smart and living her best life.

NEVER GIVE UP

God's Speed! I am thankful and blessed to say that my multi-talented son is currently completing his bachelor's degree at North Carolina State University. Despite his life setback, he was accepted at North Carolina State University with a track and field scholarship, and has become an outstanding professional athlete. He also has an entrepreneurial spirit. He is the successful owner of several businesses and living his best life.

NEVER GIVE UP

I must say, I would not have overcome my setbacks and failures without the guidance of the Holy Spirit. No matter what crazy idea I come up with or want to try, if I believe it's possible, the Holy Spirit assures me I can accomplish it. When I get tired from my demanding schedule, family problems or just life – I hear the word- *resilience.* I now know that I can do whatever I set my mind to achieve. I have balanced being a wife, mother, and entrepreneur and am living my best life!

Currently I am committed to collaborating with organizations and nonprofits to impact community needs. I am proudly an Active Real Estate Professional, Member of Iota Phi Lambda Sorority, Success Coach, and Mompreneur. Once I decide to move on a plan or idea, something inside of me clicks. The last 10 years have been a true roller-coaster experience, but I wouldn't change anything. Every experience has served as a life lesson. I feel my self-esteem has been stretched. I now strongly believe the motto- ***If you believe you can, you will!*** This vision is building a legacy for our family.

NEVER GIVE UP: TAKE ACTION!

- Think, speak, and act positively
- Be grateful
- Plan your day
- Prioritize
- Reflect and evaluate

What does resilience mean to YOU? It's never too late to start again.

A COMPILATION OF STORIES OF VICTORY

OUR STORIES
His Glory

SPEAKLIFE SERIES

For the LORD your God is the one who goes with you to fight for you against your enemies to give you victory.

Deuteronomy 20:4

Amy Timmons Miles

Amy Timmons Miles

Rev. Amy Timmons Miles was born and raised in Burlington, North Carolina. She is the youngest daughter of Henry Timmons Jr. and the late Gloria P. Timmons. She has two sons, Joseph and Joshua. She has two beautiful grandbabies, Lauryn and Kamryn. She received her B.A. degree in Religion and Christian Counseling from Liberty University. Currently she is enrolled at Carolina Christian College seeking her Masters of Divinity.

Rev. Miles preached her initial sermon, July 9, 2006. She served as an Associate Minister at Ebenezer United Church of Christ under the leadership of Rev. Dr. Larry Covington. Under his leadership she facilitated many small group studies, as well as taught Christian Education Classes. She has been a strong supporter of women and youth ministries.

Rev. Miles performed many duties under the leadership of Rev. Dr. George Pass Sr. at St Matthews AME Church in Burlington. She has organized and led conferences directed at providing women a place of freedom, worship, study and growth.

Rev. Miles is the Senior Pastor at Awakening Outreach Church Inc. formerly Immanuel Christian Center, Incorporated, in Burlington, North Carolina. She is the founder of Pursuing Wholeness Ministries; a ministry devoted to encouraging, maturing, and healing God's people. Because of her love for God and for His people, she has promised to devote her time, gifts and resources to the kingdom of God.

Rev. Miles is employed as an Commercial Accounts Manager with Piedmont Triad Insurance Agency. In her spare time, she likes to focus on her many hobbies; reading, movies, and spending quality time with family and friends.

Rev. Miles strives to aid the people of God by encouraging and inspiring them in their walk with Christ. She is in awe of the patience of God; Rev. Miles realizes that in her best effort she sometimes falls short. She is often reminded of the faithfulness of God. Her favorite scripture is ***Philippians 1:6 "Being confident of this very thing, that he which hath begun a good work in you will perform it until the day of Jesus Christ".***

In Plain Sight

P eeking out I could see her but she couldn't see me. I could see everything, however, no one saw me. The smell of the newness of the clothes surrounded me. The clothes were long enough to conceal me from mom and the world. Here she comes, I could hear her steps as she hurried across the floor, all the while asking others- had they seen me. Calling my name- "Amy, Amy, where are you?" I put my hand over my mouth and giggled at the fact she couldn't find me. I was fooling her. I knew something she didn't. I was smarter and I was in control. The longer I stayed hidden, the more the tone of her voice changed from one of concern to fear, and I could hear it. Wow, she was afraid. I popped out from behind the clothes, laughing, but the look on her face let me know I had messed up. Her facial expression was one of both gratitude and anger. Gratitude because I was alright, and anger because from her standpoint there was nothing funny about this.

In the movie, *"The Runaway Bride",* Julia Roberts plays a character that runs when it is time to say- "I do". One disgruntled bridegroom tells his side of the story in a bar, and a reporter, played by Richard Gere hears it and sets out to write a news article about the bride that runs. He arrives in the town and finds to his dismay that there is more to the story. She runs because she doesn't know who she is. She has lived her life taking care of an alcoholic father and acquiescing her wants for his needs. Her denial of self has gone on so long that she doesn't know who she is. In her relationships she takes on the likes and dislikes of the men she dates and eventually runs from the alter. Julia's character, like some of us, was hiding in plain sight. In her attempt to please those in her life, her father, her men and her friends, she loses herself in the process.

She runs from the altar for the final time only to run into herself. One of the things she adopts, as her own from every relationship, is the way the men in her life eat their eggs. When the fraud is finally exposed, she discovers that she doesn't even like eggs! She embarks on a journey to discover who she is and what she likes. When Julia Roberts' character comes out of hiding she discovers her passion, her joy and she becomes self-aware.

It amazes me how as life goes on and we grow older, the things we thought were funny in our younger years no longer are comical. We now understand the seriousness of our actions. Unfortunately, there are also some habits in our younger years that we adopt as a way of life. An innocent childhood game became the backdrop to my life. Hiding came easy to me, it wasn't something I planned or even thought of; it just happened. Whenever I felt lost, out of control, threatened, or rejected I resorted to hiding.

I was hiding in plain sight of everyone. Very few people in my life really knew the real me. I often wondered how someone could believe the worst about me. Now I know, they never really knew me. I only presented to them what I wanted them to see and know. I became an expert at concealing my wounds, my failures, my hurts, and my fears. I hid it all. Thrust into the limelight at an early age, I learned to perform and still hide. I hid the feeling I had when my Dad and Mom would argue. I hid how it made me feel when my Dad would leave me in the car and go into his friend's house. I hid my feelings of failure and rejection after two failed marriages. I hid the feelings and the fact that I was abused at nine years old. I hid the fact that I was bullied most of my life. I hid how worthless and empty I felt when a childhood friend attempted to rape me. I hid.

I was no longer hiding behind clothes in a department store, I was hiding behind a smile and laughter. As my Mom lay on her deathbed, I sat beside her and wondered what was behind her laughter. My mom had a quick wit; she made everyone around her laugh. I believe my mom was hiding too. She had her own hurts, disappointments, and failures. Had her laughter become her escape, her healing and her hiding place? Life has exposed the fraud in me.

Most of us are self-conscious but not self-aware. We are more worried about what other people think of us than about wrestling with our feelings or motivations." Shame had caused me to be more afraid of what people would think than knowing or becoming who I really am. Unfortunately, I found myself in good company; in the Bible, Jesus asked the Samaritan woman why she was at the well in the middle of day (paraphrase). Her shame caused her to be at the well, alone in the middle of day when everyone else came in the morning. So many people have been hiding because of shame, insecurities, and hurt. I had to find out why I was hiding. I've never understood the significance of the phrase "coming out of the closet," until now. The significance of it is the freedom, the relief it brings. You no longer have to hide from the world what you have known most of your life. Prior to the "coming out" you live your life to make everyone else happy. You live in fear of the repercussions of your choices; rejection, stares, and judgement. You live in fear of the cost. "I don't have to prove that I'm lovable or valuable. I don't have to be right all the time. I can be vulnerable and be myself even if others don't accept me. I can even take risks and fall."

Wow, what a discovery, to realize I am free to be me! I am so glad God came searching for me just as my Mom did. Neither allowed me to stay hidden. Now, the question to be answered is, who am I? Let me introduce myself. In order to tell you who I am I must tell you who I was. I have been insecure for as long as I can remember. I never remember a time when I was really confident. Right after my 35th High School Class Reunion, I wrote these words. "I no longer saw my classmates through the eyes of an insecure teenager full of jealousy and envy of their lives and accomplishments. Now I could look at them through the eyes of a woman; confident and secure in who she has become."

One of the by-products of hiding is I became a people-pleaser; afraid, and insecure. Whether my people-pleasing came from the abuse, being bullied or from the fact that my father was in the home but not present, I am not sure. However, I would do most anything to please the people in my life. Lie, cheat, and speak ill of people that had done me no wrong; all to fit in. I have been in relationships with people, both male and female who from the beginning didn't have my best interest at heart; that had their own agenda. And unfortunately, I had mine; to be accepted.

The second by-product of hiding is insecurity. You are never secure even though your mind tells you, you are safe in here. There is always the possibility you will be found out and exposed. Yet at all cost you hide the hurt, the emptiness, the loneliness and the pain. When I felt mistreated by others, my insecurity caused me to try to figure out why. I never looked at them, I blamed myself. When in a room with powerful women, I would shrink. I had little or no self-esteem and I allowed people to misuse me because I needed their approval. I stayed in toxic relationships because they made me feel wanted. I just wanted to be loved and accepted. That alone boggles my mind; to stay in a relationship detrimental to my well-being all for appearance sake. I have lied to myself most of all. I have hurt people I love, all because I was ashamed and afraid to take off my mask. I craved affirmation from my parents and others. I have preached the Word of God and in the same breath denying it all when it came to my own life. I have been a fraud. I could believe God for your life, I could speak into your life and I didn't have enough love for myself to believe God would do the same for me.

Like Julia Roberts' character in the "Run Away Bride," a lot of things I did were out of a sense of obligation not love. Love isn't an obligation; it is a privilege. I had to hit rock bottom to finally decide I was important, too. How I feel, my desires, my life and my dreams matter. It all matters. When Julia Robert's character steps out of the shadow of her father, being the butt of jokes in her family and in the community, she realizes she has dreams, passions and a future beyond what has happened to her. The Samaritan woman in the Bible steps out of her shadow of shame and rejection, and because of her bravery, a whole community comes to know Jesus Christ. When I stepped out of the shadows, I discovered there was a whole world that had been waiting on me. What will happen if you step out of the shadows and reveal who you really are? Who is waiting on you?

Let me introduce you to ME. I am Amy Timmons Miles. I love sweets, cakes and candy. I love to watch television, mostly movies, genre doesn't matter. I cry while watching movies. I love all the Transformer and the Furious movies. I love watching Westerns on Saturday with my Dad. I love music, any genre (not Rap so much) and I love to dance. An athlete by nature, I love to run. I find so much joy and peace in running. I love spending time with my family and my friends. My family means the world to me. To threaten them is to threaten me. I am an extrovert with a splash of introvert. I am intelligent. I am determined.

The challenges I have faced have made me who I am. I love to laugh and to see others laugh. Christmas is my favorite time of the year. I love to give gifts, whether I receive or not. To see the smiles on my family's face is enough for me. I am a sun worshipper. I love to sit out in the sun to feel the warmth of the rays. I love the beach. It is my place of zen. I love to read and sit in the quiet. I love to ride in my car; in silence no music, just me and my thoughts. I love the smile on my granddaughters' faces. That makes me happy. I miss my Mom. My Daddy's Girl status developed later in life. I was glued to my mom's side.

I am anointed by God to set the captive free. I have been appointed by God to do Kingdom work. I am His child, His preacher, His prophet, His apostle, I belong to God. I love the poem "Our Deepest Fear" by Marianne Williamson; she states, "You are a child of God. Playing it small doesn't serve the world. There's nothing enlightened about shrinking so that other people won't feel insecure around you. We are all meant to shine, as children do."

I have played small for too long, catering to feelings of others; feeding their insecurities while I lost myself in the process. I once called myself, "The Wounded Healer". I was wounded, however I am allowing God to heal my wounds. I am through playing small for people. I am through hiding behind clothes, laughter or a smile. I am who God created me to be. I am powerful beyond measure. I am confident and bold. That's who I am.

The child in me that was neglected, abused and rejected, had to allow the adult me to bring her out of hiding. No more hiding, I am UNASHAMEDLY AMY. I make no apologies, no excuses, this is ME, *IN PLAIN SIGHT*.

A COMPILATION OF STORIES OF VICTORY

OUR STORIES
His Glory

SPEAKLIFE SERIES

I have told you these things, so that in me you may have peace. In this world you will have trouble. But take heart! I have overcome the world.

John 16:33

Jermain Smith

Jermain Smith

Jermain Smith is the founder & CEO of Smith Prudent Reads, LLC and the "Dream Big" author and illustrator of the children's book series- *Brooklyn Astronaut (TM)*. He is involved with reading his books in the schools in the community, and plans to start a nonprofit organization in the near future. Jermain's passion is to work through after-school programs to teach children about business and entrepreneurship. His goal is to motivate children to view entrepreneurship as a viable way to secure a prosperous future and live out their best dreams. Jermain believes that he can use his book series and his workshops on business and entrepreneurship to help our youth create new visions of their future, instead of getting caught up and wasting their lives in the streets.

My Shelter Experience

On February 24, 1991, weighing exactly 10 pounds, I was born into the world. While being pregnant with me, my mother was involved in a major car accident. This caused major complications in my mother's pregnancy. Due to the pain from the accident she had to take pain-killers and was told by her doctors that I would not have a healthy birth. The doctors reported that I would be both physically deformed and mentally retarded, and would have to spend the majority of my life in a mental institution. Six doctors strongly recommended that my mother get an abortion and they refused to do the birth delivery. Stuck between a rock and a hard place, my mother turned to her Christian faith and committed herself to fasting and praying to the Lord. The seventh doctor was one of faith, who told my mother- " If you believe in God for your child, I will do the birth delivery. Due to my large size, my mother had a cesarean section and the doctor had to dislocate my shoulder to get me out of my mother's womb. As my medical reports came back, the doctors were all astonished. I was healthy and had no physical deformities or mental retardation. This was my struggle entering into the world.

Fast forward to my struggle as a teenager. I was assaulted by a street gang known as the Bloods. I was not a member of a gang, just an innocent high school student who became a victim in the gang's attempt to rob me. I was bleeding from the top right part of my skull from a deadly blow to the head with a gun while being shot from behind by the other two gang bangers involved. One gang member shot me, while the other shouted out, "run those pockets," as he patted down my jean pockets for money. I was unconscious, laying lifeless in the school hallway. Opening up my eyes in the school office, the first thing I heard as I was violently being shaked to wake up was- " I can't feel a pulse; he is dead." I then spent the next two years sleeping 18 hours a day, in complete physical and emotional torment and agony, with no relief or comfort. I took 8-12 over the counter pain-killers a day to deal with the pain because the doctors couldn't heal me. I sustained a brain injury and suffered damage to my inner ear. My tragedy continued from my teenage years to my early adulthood with more pain and woes.

I have had two bowel obstructions which once again created torment and pain in my body. My bowels were on the verge of bursting inside of my body and the doctors rushed me in for emergency surgery. Even with seven shots of morphine, the pain refused to leave. Just before the doctors were going to perform the surgery to stop the internal swelling from bursting and emptying inside my blood stream, I was able to go to the restroom.

I became a drug dealer during those years of my affliction. I started selling and using drugs to cope with feeling broken and hopeless with no future. I have done marijuana, cocaine, ecstasy, molly colada pills; every drug that I could get my hands on to numb the pain. Drugs were my escape from my reality and my suicidal thoughts of wanting to die. I was on a very dark path, all of my friends at the time where drug dealers and goons. One day the Lord arrested me and I became demon-possessed. I saw a snake trying to suffocate me, to eat me alive and rats talking to me. I heard the voice of the enemy taunting me. My mother called one of the members of the church and they prayed for me for about three to four hours. I was foaming at the mouth and my skin became purple. I felt like I was losing physical control of my body. After the prayers, the Lord spoke to me and I heard birds singing. In my mind, I saw streaming water by a huge, beautiful tree and there was a bright, pure white light that permeated the scene. I also heard the water babbling like a spring. Finally, I was able to go to sleep. The Lord instructed me to write a relationship book and revealed to me revelations on relationships and love. That process of starting to write my books, took me out of the streets; away from the negative crowd that I was rolling with.

I was told twice by my father that I was worthless. The first time was when I started smoking marijuana to deal with the pain of my assault when it first happened. The second time was when my father was sick. Initially I did not know which hospital he was in. Once I discovered his location, I was preparing to go visit him. He came home early, and made sure to tell me what he thought about me not getting there fast enough to visit him. I confronted him, explained the situation that had prevented me from getting to the hospital sooner and told him to apologize. He never did. However, through God's grace, I forgave him and moved on with my life. I began a habit of writing ten minutes a day, and with medicine, my disability became more regulated and I was able to perform more effectively.

I wrote my book and I ended up meeting a New York Times best-selling author. After I got out of the street life, most of my family were never happy or supportive of my dreams of making a better life for myself. Only my mother was consistently supportive and loving of me and my dreams. My mother insisted that I try to create a bond with my father. As a result of my mother's encouragement, I made one more attempt to invite my father back in my life. My father was very cold. I was so excited to be working with this New York Times best-selling author, and when I brought the good news to my father, he sat there on the couch, not lifting up his head, and said- " just because he is successful, don't mean you'll be." I was so shocked and taken aback that I quietly left the living room.

Things went south in the business deal with the New York Times best-selling author, and I was crushed by the whole experience. Somehow, I found the strength through the encouragement from a business colleague, to not give up. Over time, I started my own publishing company and secured my limited liability company status (LLC). My second book, which I authored and illustrated was a children's book called *Brooklyn Astronaut*. I did a commercial, and got great responses from the community and especially from my mother. I had my brother's daughter and son in the commercial. Later, I was told by my niece that I was working them like slaves and she and her brother demanded pay. It had always been my intention to pay them for their participation in the commercial. I was alarmed that my niece and nephew would think that I would take advantage of them. I found out that my own brother had put this poison in their heads. I was in disbelief that my brother would create this situation. It was both upsetting and hurtful. Of course I paid my niece and nephew what I could. I seemed to always have money or cash flow issues because my income was below the poverty level. I was barely bringing in $10,000 a year and was living at my mother's house at the time.

My sister also told my mother that I was wasting my life on that "stupid book". That "stupid book", as my sister called it, took me out of the streets and provided a future for me. The envy and jealousy of my family members grew worse and worse. My mother kept encouraging me in my dreams and her strength helped me to continue. I managed to get an investor to fund my enrollment in a program with a famous sponsorship coach that taught me how to write corporate sponsorship proposals, including a contract for sponsorship within her digital class. That's when all hell broke loose. Using a permanent marker, my cousin vandalized a pair of shoes that had been given to me by my brother. My brother warned me that my relatives were conspiring against me to get me out of the family inheritance. He warned me to watch my back.

Considering the fact that my brother and none of my family, except my mother, had shown me any type of emotional support previously, I decided to heed my brother's warning. One day, I saw my cousin leaving my room with a makeup kit and although I found it somewhat odd, I didn't think much of it. My spirit knew that among my cousins, hatred for me was developing due to my small success with my business. Affirmation came that same night when I had a dream that one of my cousins was stabbing me in my sleep.

The next morning, my spiritual conviction was once again affirmed when there was makeup on my shirt in the pattern of knife slashes. In addition, money had been taken out of my jean pants while I had been sleeping. My social security card and other important items were missing. I knew exactly where I had placed these items and now they were gone. All of my jeans were destroyed and vandalized. The coat that my mother gave me for Christmas had the fur cut up from the hoodie; it was hanging in the back of my closet. This was more than upsetting. When one of my cousins, that moved out of the house returned, I decided to go upstairs into the extra vacant apartment because I felt that I was on the verge of a mental breakdown. I wanted to avoid the trouble and harassment of having to interact with this cousin. But my father came upstairs, after ignoring the signs of me being wrongly provoked, and ordered me to come down stairs. Which I refused to do because I wanted to avoid any more sabotage until my cousin left. My father called the police. This was too much, I was provoked beyond my limits and my nerves became highly irritated.

I spent the next two days in the *crazy* house. Upon leaving the care facility, I spent the night in the abandoned building my parents were on the verge of selling. It was in the dead cold of winter; I slept on the bare floor in my winter coat that was insufficient to keep me warm. I had been kicked out of the house by my father, I was disabled and I had nowhere to go. The next day I went and checked myself into the shelter system. I had no choice. I got really sick while being in the shelter because my insurance was denied and therefore, I wasn't covered to receive my physical therapy.

My mother called one night, crying and begging me to come back home, but my relatives were so wicked to me that I couldn't return. I comforted my mother and told her that God would make a way. While being homeless I lived off the food stamps and shelter food. I gave my entire disability check to my sponsorship coach who was working on getting me sponsored with my proposal. Every night coming into the shelter, I was treated like a criminal. The staff searched me every night and I had to go through a metal detector.

We had to sneak food in our locker just to have something to eat during the night. I often shared and made peanut butter and jelly sandwiches for me and the other men sleeping in my dorm. On my birthday my father and brother called to take me out. My brother, knowing that I was homeless, asked me in front of his business coworkers where I was living. I knew he was trying to embarrass me. In anger I responded that I was staying with a friend, but that I was working on getting into a condo. My father held his head down as I made the comment. Everyone was surprised by what I said. For some strange reason they actually believed me.

In my mind, I was hoping to use a portion of my sponsorship money to get a nice place to live. My mother thought I had told my father and brother about the sponsorship. I explained to her that I would never tell them. It would only make things worse.

I remember attending church during this time. I had dropped out of the choir due to the shelter curfew. No one in the church ever reached out to see what was going on with me or to even try and build a Christian friendship with me. During one Sunday morning service, the assistant pastor preached and shared that the holy spirit spoke to him, saying that- "someone in the church is homeless and no one knows, but that person wouldn't be homeless for long". I immediately broke down and started to cry as other people came forth and gave their testimony about how God provided them a lease for their apartment after they had gone through being homeless. I started to worship and praise God and everyone gave me weird looks as if to say- "what's wrong with him", but I kept praising God and the spirit herself spoke to me and said- *"I am going to give you a condo with a view."* I heard those exact words right after the pastor spoke in that worship service. Three weeks later, my caseworker called me into the shelter office and told me that I was randomly selected for housing and that I won the lottery for housing! After spending seven months in the shelter, I finally got to view the apartment that the Lord provided for me. It was truly a dream come true for me. I always wanted to live in a condo and the view on the rooftop was so breathtaking and inspiring. Though all my tribulations, adversity, and fiery trials, the Lord stayed true to His promise. I may not be where I want to be in my business as of yet, but to have a roof over my head and a beautiful place to live that is nontoxic is exactly what I needed, and I am so grateful to God for his grace, mercy and favour on my life. Sometimes in the dark moments in our life, we may not understand why we are suffering. But, if we hold on to our faith, I am a witness that the Lord will bring us out victorious. And I know that God's love is all I need in this world, to make it through. My shelter experience was one that I hated, but it was the stepping stone for God bringing this *ghetto child* into a healthy and prosperous place of light!

Laticia Nicole Beatty

Laticia Nicole Beatty

Laticia Nicole Beatty is a certified life coach, motivational speaker, bestselling author, independent business owner, and founder of a non-profit organization, Purposed Professionals Inc. But, most importantly she is a child of the Almighty God and is on a mission to encourage and transform people out of dead situations with her #Speaklife Enterprises. La'Ticia has been on stages across the country inspiring audiences from all backgrounds.

With a heart to serve, Tish, as she is often called, received a BS in Nursing from Winston-Salem State University and a Masters in Business Administration from the University of Phoenix. She is currently a full time Minister and Life Coach.

La'Ticia Nicole Beatty's greatest accomplishments are her marriage to her husband, Antonio for nearly 21 years and their two children, Antonio II and Aden Cole.

Some Accomplishments/Awards
2013 Humanitarian Award
2014 Executive Director of the Year Award
2016 ACHI Mentor of the Year Award
2016 Spiritual Woman Award
2016 Author of the Year Award
2016 Devotional of the Year Indie Author Legacy Award
2016 God Phenomenal Woman Honor
2017 Woman of the Year Community Service Award
2018 Marketing Director of the Year Award
2019 Diamond of the Year Award
2019 Triumph Woman of Distinction Award

Laticia Nicole #Speaklife
www.LaticiaNicole.com

The Production Power of Pain

Are you really being a good mom, a good wife, a good director, a good minister, or are you hyper-focusing on the hats you wear to avoid the hurts you bear? I asked myself this question.

I was at home on my computer trying to write this book when the realization hit me, and I had to stop. I wasn't telling the whole story. That's not to say that I was lying, because I wasn't. I was holding back, just enough to be on the side of victorious rather than victimized. It was essentially the same thing I'd done in my first book, which has yet to be published. It was getting too real. My first book, I didn't even publish because there was so much pain in it. I blamed so many people for what I was feeling—the rapists, the molesters, the people that made fun of me, my cousins that picked on me. I couldn't publish that book. People wouldn't talk to me to this day. So, I stored it away and published something safer instead.

The most shocking lightbulb click, though, was realizing that not only am I holding back on paper, but I'm standing in the way of my healing. I'm not dealing with my pain. I'm hiding it in production. Instead of dealing with the things that are hurting me, I produce something else to be proud of. I knew it was something I dealt with as a child wanting approval, then again as a college student who studied hard to prove everyone wrong who said I'd amount to nothing but a stripper. I realized that day though, that my issue of needing to prove myself worthy wasn't past tense. It was still a current issue.

Since 2014, I've amassed over 100 awards. That's a proud moment, no doubt, but if you zoom in a little closer, you'll see that I also started writing my first book, the unpublished one, about a year before the avalanche of awards. In that untold story, I wrote about things like being ridiculed, molested, assaulted, and almost losing my life. I'd successfully tucked those memories and feelings away for so long, now here they were in my face again. Although I didn't publish that particular book, I released another in addition to working my behind off on the job. It was my way of evading emotions that didn't feel good.

I didn't have to think about childhood trauma and how it's still affecting me at work. My career gave me space to be and do something that felt positive. Why subject myself to pain when promotions are on the table? Within a year of realizing that the sexual abuse I dealt with as a girl was still affecting me as a woman, I was named Executive Director of the Year on my job. I saw that I was still being distressed by the past trauma, but I never gave myself time to see *how* it was bothering me and what was needed, beyond prayer, to finally relinquish its hold on me.

There's a similar instance in my marriage. I've been married for twenty-one years this year. As I evaluate the changes and the things that have gone on earlier in my marriage, I didn't deal with it. I didn't deal with stuff, period. I just wrote a book or went and got another degree. I keep producing all this stuff, because I have not shared a lot of my story. I can't free myself from it, because I keep it bottled in. I recently wrote a children's book, which was my way of overcoming feeling ugly and being talked about. Being told I'm shaped funny, that I look funny, that my hair is too short. I had to go back to that child and tell her she was beautiful. My name is Laticia which means joy. The little girl in my book is named Joy. That was me.

The book does a wonderful job of affirming self-love and self-acceptance in little Laticia who needed those words back in the day and to other little girls across the world who still need those words today. But did I really deal with the issue of feeling ugly? I have to ask myself because I've mastered the ability of hiding pain under production, not really dealing with it purposely.

God said what the enemy meant for bad, he can use for your good, that your pain will lead to your purpose. But are we really truly healing through the pain or are we clapping through it? Until we truly heal from our pain, it'll keep showing up. It's like a migraine. You can pop pills all day long to deal with the symptoms, but until you address the root of the issue, the headaches will keep coming back. That's the case with me. It went from sexual abuse and emotional neglect to ridicule and threats against my life, poverty, substance abuse, infidelity, and the list goes on. It wasn't the same pain, but I was still using the same coping mechanism—overachieving—to deal with pain.

Overachieving is an addiction, more specifically it's a mental health condition that's rooted in coping with trauma—as most addictions are. It can be just as physically, mentally and socially unhealthy as an addiction to drugs, alcohol, and sex. The biggest difference, however, is that overachieving is praised by society. The Enneagram personality test shows me to be an Enthusiast. It says that we're optimistic, versatile, and spontaneous. Who wouldn't want to embody these characteristics? I'm the Nursing Home Administrator, Entrepreneur, Company Top 5 Marketing Director, community philanthropist and the model signed with two agencies. I'm the writer with five books. I'm the CEO, coach, minister, and praise team leader. I am so many things. I am the mom and wife. Overachievers are often labeled as Type A personalities, go-getters, ambitious, winners, role models, and all of these other glamorous labels. Yet, the other side of the classification is rarely talked about.

Overachieving has cost me my friendships. Understandably, my friends stopped inviting me out, because I rarely showed up. I'm too busy producing and I overextend myself. And because I resort to working in place of dealing with my *stuff*, it's keeping me from being the greater me. The greatest version of ourselves is in alignment. When we're in alignment, everything is well—our mind, body, spirit, finances, and relationships. My scale is constantly tipping too far to the left then too far to the right. Until I learn to say- "that hurt" and not try to rush past that feeling with a longer to-do list, then I'll continue to be out of alignment.

Because the win isn't grounded in alignment and pure intention, the joy is stripped from it. Yeah, I might be happy for the moment, but that's fleeting. It's like a high. I'm high and happy, then I come down and am in search of the next high. It's an extreme. Joy, on the other hand, is more of a constant. Its foundation is that place of alignment. And when the achievement isn't built from a foundation of alignment, there's no joy in it, only quickly fleeting happiness. Everybody looking at you like you made it, but you think, "I haven't done anything. I haven't gone anywhere. What do you mean congratulations?"

Then there are the scoffs or the *hmpf*s. When you win a lot and make a lot of money, a lot of people won't like you. They only want to clap for so long. It's cute until you go above the person who brought you in. The *hmpf*s would say things online like, "I don't have to have ABCDEFG behind my name to make money," and I'd know they were talking about me because I have an RN, BSN, NHA, MBA, and I'm working on my doctorate. This isn't uncommon. More broadly, we refer to these *hmpf*s as haters; they hate on you because they want what you have.

The more they spoke against me on social media (trying to make me come out of myself), the more $10k bonuses I bonused! Instead of dealing with the negative emotions of them talking about me and making wise cracks, I'd go above and beyond. Instead of reverting to the person I could be or used to be, which is precisely what they want me to do, I bonus another $10k. That still wasn't dealing with the pain though, because it still hurt to be talked about and looked at as being odd or different. The issue has less to do with them and far more to do with me, because why are they bothering me? Whenever something gets under your skin to that degree, there's a deeper issue in the heart to be addressed. That means there's some past trauma lurking around in there. As a leader in any community or field, you have to expect to be talked about. It comes with the territory. They talked about Jesus! Why wouldn't they talk about me?

The problem with envy and jealousy, however, is that you never know what the person is dealing with. You see the material things, but you know nothing of process. For instance, I told my pastor before that I don't have an outlet. I can't just let go. I have to be on my P's and Q's at all times, because I'm a leader. In church, I'm a leader. So, do I get a chance to just be? At my house, I am the wife and mother. We're raising strong men, so that means I need to be strong. I have coaches and mentors, but they're hard on me. I don't get the chance to just be weak. I don't get to just scream. People expect more out of the tough ones. But I'm human. We're human.

Sometimes people think just because you made it to the other side alive, you're okay. Yeah, that's victory, but you still must deal with the actual process. We want to say "hooray, they made it through the wilderness. They made it to the promised land." But we don't want to talk about all the people that got bit by snakes, the people that didn't make it, all the things you've seen. It does affect us. I'll bring it back to my life. We cheer that I made it, but I can't talk about how many men touched me, how many times I've been beaten, how many times I've been shot at, how many people I've stabbed. Yeah, I made it, but just because I can put makeup on it, the scars are still there.

The scars tell the stories that I don't want to. I can slap some foundation and blush on top of it and forget for a second that they're there, but soon as I kick off the heels and wash my face, the scars are still there. Those horrible things happened to me. I can't separate myself from my past. It's a part of who I am. But while I might respond to my hurt these days by producing something beautiful, I didn't always do that. Once upon a time, I solidified my heart and I don't ever want to be her again. She was heartless. She didn't care. I've gone through that version of myself and I don't ever want to go through that again, yet looking too closely at my scars in the mirror scares me sometimes, I fear that I just might spiral back down into that cold, heartless place of pain.

The God of the promise is the same God of the process. Overcoming adversity does not have to be dreadful. That's Satan making us believe anything different. That's Satan telling me that I can trust my ability to produce, create and achieve, but that I shouldn't trust myself to look in the mirror and deal with what I see, lest I spiral down in drowning emotions. But God said in Isaiah 43:1, *Fear not, for I have redeemed you. I have called you by name. You are mine.*

Fear not: Release that fear of missing out. If you don't do it all right now, you'll miss out. If you don't write the book, do the cruise, do the conference, preach on Friday, speak on Monday…you're not good enough. None of that is true.

For I have redeemed you: You're the only one holding you back. Your fear of letting go and surrendering is keeping you captive, yet you've already been redeemed. You're just waiting on you.

I have called you by name: He didn't call your mother or your father, your grandparents, your children, your spouse. He called you by your name. Your why is you, no one else.

You are mine: He's claimed you—you and everything you've gone through. He's seen it all and none of it made Him turn His back on you. You have no reason to live in shame or secrecy.

The first stage of addressing the problem is the acknowledgement. The Enthusiast can be just as scatter-brained, impulsive, and overextending as we are ambitious, high-spirited and practical. I knew that but didn't care. I knew my overachieving was costing me valuable relationships, but I just kept running from one thing to another. Now I'm in stage 2, where I realize that something is missing because I'm never satisfied. I'm beginning to ask myself more questions: What is it going to take to just slow down, process, and finish? What that looked like for me, was going through a painful situation, processing it, producing something out of it, then patting my own self on the back. I did this for myself and for the glory of God, not to prove anything to anyone else.

Now I challenge you to ask yourself why, and your why can't be a who. It can't be your children. Let's talk about the *who* being *you*. Let's talk about *you*. Why are you pursuing the goals that you are? Why are you on the go? *Is your production coming from the power of your pain?*

A COMPILATION OF STORIES OF VICTORY

OUR STORIES
His Glory

SPEAKLIFE SERIES

Therefore put on the full armor of God, so that when the day of evil comes, you may be able to stand your ground, and after you have done everything, to stand.

Ephesians 6:13

Lisa Jones Stanton

Lisa Jones Stanton

Lisa Jones Stanton recently retired after 35 years in the automotive industry. Lisa has found a new passion/calling/career as a financial strategist, working to improve the financial lives of families to God's Glory. A native of Ohio, she transplanted to Michigan to attend college in the 1980's. She is a wife, mother of three adult children, and grandmother to one beautiful granddaughter.

Lisa received her B.S degree from General Motors Institute (Kettering University) and M.S. degree from the University of Michigan; both in Industrial Engineering. She spent over 40 years in the automotive industry. She rose to the position of an Engineering Manager in Program Management. She mentored and guided many young people in their careers. She successfully led the Women in Product Development Mentoring Circle for over 13 years. In 2017, Lisa was a recipient of the Women of Color Technology All-Star Award. After she retired, Lisa began a new career, becoming licensed and certified in financial services.

Lisa is the Founder and CEO of Financial Fitness for Freedom, a complete financial services business with an unique approach, in that she helps people find retirement money they lose unknowingly or unnecessarily. Thus, providing for their financial future by delivering financial education, college planning, retirement planning, and tax planning.

In her role as a financial strategist, Lisa is a member of the Western Washtenaw Business Association and Power Through Networking. She is a community volunteer with Gleaners Food Bank, Ronald MacDonald House, and the Washtenaw and South Eastern Michigan United Ways; serving as a Vita tax preparer, mentor, and financial supporter. Lisa is a blossoming speaker, motivator and author.

Lisa shares her story with individuals who are experiencing life and financial challenges, and she spends her time mentoring women and young people. Her goal is to help 20,000 individuals, with "creating your forever money". In her downtime, she loves traveling, hanging with her grand-daughter, water aerobics, all kinds of really good food, and understanding financial history.

Connect with Lisa:

Follow her on Facebook and Instagram at:
Facebook: facebook.com/Lisa Jones Stanton
Instagram: Lisastanton5@outlook.com

For a financial consultation: call/text (725) 333-5675
Email: Financialfitnessforfreedom@gmail.com
Financialfitnessforfreedom.com
For a phenomenal business opportunity visit me at:
https://LisaStanon.FreedomEquityGroup.com

The Cure Became The Addiction

I can't believe this is happening again!

I cry out holding my head in my hands. What's the definition of insanity: Doing the same thing over and over, but expecting a different result? I believed when this happened two months ago, I figured out the solution, never go to the *casino alone*. But somehow here I am again, *alone,* and having lost my new carpet, or my next two vacations or another bill fully paid.

The backstory - When I was asked to be part of this book, I had no idea what I was going to write about. I had a remarkable life. I had to go back and add the *seemingly*. I had a *seemingly* remarkable life. On the outside looking in, my life was impressive. I had been married almost 30 years, worked for over 30 years for a Detroit major automotive company, had three healthy kids, and one beautiful granddaughter. The kids were making their way and no longer living in my pocket; they only occasionally visited my pocket. I had a great job. I liked it except for the near proximity politics. I had risen through the ranks to mid-management. You know mid-management, where you're asked to walk on water so your boss can take credit for your miracle. At various times in my career I was one of a few if not the only black female at this level of management. Although I wasn't paid as well as my white male counterparts, I was still paid very well. My position at work and the money I made, defined my self-worth. Not in the way most people think, but in a good way. I was giving to my employees and the other groups to which I volunteered my time. I had no issue taking the team out for a five hundred dollars lunch or getting together with the extended family and buying dinner for everyone, or at least those who made significantly less than me. I freely loaned or gave money to help those in need. I hope this was never viewed as a power thing but as generosity. I felt if all my bills were paid and the credit cards were not maxed out, I'd eventually get caught up. I believed that if they were in my shoes, they would do the same for me.

Once I was out of college, my focus was on dining out and shopping. From the beginning of my career, I always worked long hours. I started my career as a production supervisor on the line, working twelve hours per day, six days a week and eight hours on Sunday. I deserved to spend money, go out to dinner, buy clothes, furniture, and go on vacation. I lived alone and most of the time I ate alone. The workers in the restaurants and the clerks in the store became my companions. When I went out to dinner, I could have a good meal in the company of others even if I was sitting alone. I also had waiters and waitresses to talk to. And sometimes I'd sit at the bar, what's a meal without a cocktail. And bartenders are great conversationalists. When shopping, you can talk to a clerk on a slow weeknight for hours. I was new to the area and had too demanding a work schedule to develop real friendships; I guess you'd say I bought my friends.

After the kids arrived, I still routinely worked fifty-five to sixty hours per week. I felt like I owed the kids good vacations, Disney World and Disneyland. This included more dining out. No meals to prepare, kitchen to clean, and dishes to do. Or kids whining, "do we have to have this again?". Or my all-time favorite, "I don't do re-runs" (leftovers). The shopping bug transformed into the hunt- for- bargains specialist in order to cloth my three kids and myself. I was still in the stores, but spending less. Once again, I deserved it and I could afford it. All the bills were paid, and the credit cards were not maxed out.

As my kids got older, it was nice vacations, braces, jewelry, cars and fancy graduation parties. And then one day, the house was quiet. I was once again eating my meals alone and what fun was that? I'd invite others to dinner or hangout with my favorite waitress or bartender. My husband and I had really developed separate lives. I never realized how separate our lives had become until the kids were gone. To bring us back together, we started having a date night during the week. This typically consisted of dinner and the casino, which in the beginning was fine. Between us, we might gamble a hundred dollars; win gas money or lose and go home. Then one day, the worst possible thing that can happen to a gambler happened to us, we turned that hundred dollars into a couple of thousand dollars. We were both hooked. Now I know how an addict feels. Like any addiction it starts slow and escalates. My husband and I were good addicts; before gambling we made sure all our bills were always paid, and we had deposited our savings for retirement. My husband was gambling from a zero-debt position. I was not. I had plenty of debt from my previous addictions of dining out, shopping and traveling. I rationalized that I was a manager, and I should live like one. Money was a great cure for loneliness, but ultimately it became the addiction.

Slowly date nights fell away. We no longer gambled at the same table. We developed different styles of play. My husband became a high-stake hit- and- run player. I became a sit- down- get comfy and play- for- hours player. I was that player who enjoyed chatting with the dealers and the other players. The time my husband and I spent together became less and less. With the stress of a withering, uncertain marriage, and the stress of the job, trips to the casino became the routine. It was only a fifteen-minute drive from work. Home was further. I'd go most Wednesdays for the *free* gifts and dinner, one other random day, but definitely every Friday to decompress after a long week. I'd enjoy happy hour at one of the casinos, then start playing for mindless hours. Most of the time, I wasn't there to win, I was just there to play for six to ten hours. Sometimes, I'd win immediately and wouldn't stop. The need for validation and the need to fight away loneliness are *huge monsters*. Through my journey, I have come to respect all addicts. Gambling involves no illegal drugs, but the natural endorphin high in the brain is as real as the high from any drug. The physical desire, not just the mental desire, to participate and be involved is as real as an addict's need for drugs. I can't tell you how many times I've said, "I can't believe I lost so much, again. You'll get it back next time". Gambling calls you and you give in; you need a fix.

Time in the casino became more and more time alone, without my husband. But it was the casino that provided my last positive memory of togetherness with my husband, so for that reason it was comforting. Sometimes I would stay at the casino for the conversations instead of heading home when I should have. For me, gambling was stress- free and mindless. And it comes with perks; the dealers and pit bosses know your name. Waitresses come up to you and say, do you want the usual? Valets ask you about your kids. Gambling becomes a safe haven to help fight the loneliness. It makes you feel special until you've lost all your money. Money that was planned to cover something else. But it can be an amazing way to fight loneliness and to lift your self-esteem. When you can take a hundred dollars and turn it into a few thousand dollars, you feel like a king or queen. But when you lose, it feels like the **life was sucked out of you**. You tell yourself, "You can get it back". That declaration starts an unbreakable cycle of perpetual winning and losing, of course, more losing than winning. Borrowed money, savings, and credit cards, and something you, non-gamblers, don't know about, the *marker*. A *marker* is a revolving loan from a casino, there's no interest for thirty days and then you pay it back or they reach into your checking account and take it. A *marker* is the ultimate way to lose track of what you're really spending, no money out of your pocket and chip denominations that are only distinguishable by color. If the chips were weighted, at least there would be a physical indication in the denomination, you'd know when you increased your beat. My *marker* made me feel special; not everyone can get one. The *marker* I had in Vegas, delivered three to four nights' stay at the hotel every month; anytime I wanted them. If they didn't see me for a couple of months, I actually got a call. I got free drinks, food, and limos to and from the airport. However, best of all, the dealers, pit bosses, and waitresses knew my name. I was greeted with hugs and kisses even if I was just strolling through the aisles. I was comfortable traveling to my Vegas casino alone. Once I was there, it was like hanging out with family and friends.

Before I start talking to you about the awesomeness of God...

Here's a Public Service Announcement:

1) Nothing is *Free* in the Casino: Repeat after me. Five times- Nothing is *Free* in the Casino.

2) No matter how the casino looks after you, the casino only cares about getting your *money*. No one there is your friend unless they were your friend before you started gambling. I'd need another half chapter to demonstrate, *pleasssssse* just trust me.

#

Now, let's talk about the awesomeness of God! I'm a work-in-progress, not completely healed but at least I recognize the money cure has become the disease; the addiction. What has God done for me? He quietly started transforming my life. God is sneaky. I was going about my crazy, out-of-control life with the façade of looking in control. And God starts bringing order, putting people and things in my life that will transform it. For instance, out of nowhere someone asked me to participate in a book compilation. I said okay, but what do I write about? I don't have a powerful testimony. "My life is good", the façade tells me. Then I listened to other people's stories and the onion peeling started. God blesses me with a gambling experience so bad I must cry out- "I'm a good person. Why did you let this happen to me?" God says- "Lisa, I need you to recognize who you are, how far you've come and share your story". You still have a way to go, but look how far I've brought you. You didn't even notice". God wants us to notice and to share our transformation.

The quiet transformation started about four years ago when I moved to a new job. I whined to one of my employees about my Friday night task of cleaning my house. She invited me to hang-out one Friday and have dinner together. Since the job move, my weekly schedule was less demanding and my Fridays at work were stress- free. The casino was no longer the *absolute* it had been for three years. Long story short, the person I worked with was at a restaurant that I frequented. We chatted and decided to get together the following Friday. We hit it off and started hanging-out a couple Fridays every month; trying new restaurants, or just chatting at her house. Then my daughter needed help with my

55

granddaughter after school on Wednesdays. And there went most of my Wednesdays! Recall, I went to the casino two weekdays and every Friday. Now instead of three times a week, I'm only going two to three times a month by myself. If I went more, it was with friends for dinner and *light* playing. I still went to Vegas once every three months, alone for some heavy- duty playing.

In 2018, I was offered an opportunity to retire. I took a few retirement classes, typically offered to people fifty-five or older at the community college. I thought I had done well preparing for retirement despite my wasteful spending and gambling addictions through the years. I always contributed to my 401K. I was one of the fortunate few. I had a pension. Based on the two big myths about retirement: 1) You need less money in retirement, and 2) you'll pay less taxes. I figured I was well prepared to retire. In the class, I learned I was wrong. But trust me, once you mentally decide to retire, there's no going back. I was so disgusted about the money I had wasted and the future money I would lose. I started reading books and attending every twenty-five dollars or less retirement seminar. Then I decided, I can teach others what I learned. From out of nowhere, I found a passion and a career I never knew I was interested in! Between classes, studying, and talking to prospective clients, I no longer had time or interest in local casinos. I no longer think about going to a casino except when I'm in Vegas.

The story started with, "I can't believe I'm in this situation again". Being free of addiction is indeed a process. Not too long ago, I travelled to Vegas to take my granddaughter to spend a few days with her cousin. I was on my own. I did not adhere to my new rule - I can't go to Vegas without a friend. I lose control when I'm alone. Looking back, I now realize that God helped me when I didn't fully understand the depth of my addiction. He put people and passions in my life to replace the loneliness. I am still a work in progress. In full transparency, I confess that I had a relapse one day, last month. I was at the casino and lost a small amount of money. Then I got into the *chasing game,* and didn't leave with my friends. I did not follow my new rules and as a result, I lost thousands. But through my own struggles, addictions, and loneliness, I am uniquely qualified to help others be better than me while continuing to improve myself.

There are spenders, savers and wealth creators. I was none of those, I was a waster. I love the new passion God put in my heart. I use it to help wasters become spenders, spenders become savers and savers become wealth creators. God started my transformation when I wasn't paying attention. God is Powerful, Loving, Kind, Generous and even Punitive when necessary. Sometimes, you need to be in a position where your head is in your hands and you are crying out, in order to recognize HIS Magnificent power. I resolve to take the blessing he's given me and help others. This life, this transformation, this story, and my desire to educate as many people as possible to discover the money they are losing unnecessarily and unknowingly, is to God's Glory. My goal is to improve the financial lives of twenty-thousand families. If God can change me without me even realizing it, then I have no doubt I'll reach my goal.

GOD can do anything; He knows your heart. He can change you when you're not even paying attention!

Melanie Smiles

Melanie Smiles

Melanie Smiles is a Michigan native, divorced mother of two adult children, and a grandmother. She is an author, registered nurse with 10 years of experience, specializing in emergency and trauma nursing. She is also a licensed cosmetologist, Surge365 travel member, and business owner of Mindful Missions Health and Wellness.

Melanie is a God-fearing, fun- loving, giving, caring, and nurturing woman with a gift to serve. She's triumphed through the struggles of being a high school teenage mother of two children and survivor of narcissistic abuse.

Melanie has always been hardworking, devoted to her craft, and maintained a willingness to persevere and seek growth. She is a member and serves in the nursing ministry at Peoples Community Baptist Church in Westland, Michigan. She loves to cook, travel, and spend time with her grandson, family, and friends. She has an unwavering desire to be a woman of influence by inspiring, and encouraging others to heal, overcome brokenness, and live a more peaceful, and fulfilled life. Melanie seeks to achieve this by sharing the good works of Jesus Christ.

Mindfulmission19@gmail.com
www.surge365.com/smilestours
248-688-6021
Instagram mel_rnsmiles
Facebook: Melanie Smiiles

Beautifully Broken

W e all can agree that brokenness hurts, no doubt, right? The pain we endure can be indescribable and can take on many forms. I didn't experience real heartbreak or understand brokenness until I encountered an experience that led me to write this story. I've been hurt and suffered heartaches many times in my life. However, a heartache versus heartbreak (brokenness) is different to me.

Both are emotional responses to a problem or stress. A heartache to me, is similar, to a stubbed toe, or paper cut. The pain is short lived, minimal damage, and doesn't persist. Heartbreak (brokenness) on the other hand is an overwhelming sense of seemingly never-ending, excruciating pain, felt in your heart, spirit, flesh, and can cause major damage. It can take on many forms like depression, anxiety, bitterness, shame, addiction, unhealthy behavior patterns, and suicidal and homicidal ideations.

I grew up in a two-parent Christian household and was raised by a God- fearing, praying, loving, and supportive family. As a child, I was raised in church and baptized at an early age. I knew God but didn't have a consistent relationship with him. Although I had a praying family, and was taught to pray about everything, my prayer life wasn't that strong. Most of the time I waited until bedtime to pray my traditional prayers of "Now I lay me down to sleep," or the Lord's Prayer, along with any prayer requests. I occasionally read the bible and memorized scriptures, but I didn't know the importance of it.

If I can be honest, I really didn't know how to use the bible, understand what I was reading, or know how to apply it to my life. At age fourteen visiting a friend's church, I encountered an experience I will never forget. That experience confirmed the Holy Spirit was real, and I no longer thought the older ladies in church, jumping around yelling -"Hallelujah" were faking the Holy Ghost. During prayer and worship, I had this unexplained force of energy penetrate through my body. If I had to describe the feeling, it was a gentle approach that suddenly became a powerful, overwhelming, rush of wind penetrating my soul, unconscious, but conscious mind that had me crying like a baby, and experiencing an involuntary lack of control of my tongue, words, and body. That encounter lasted every bit of five minutes, but felt like an hour. Afterwards, I entered this calming phase; still crying, I had mixed emotions of fear, and relief. The fear was from not knowing what was happening to me, and that I encountered the presence of the Holy Spirit.

Throughout the years I still wrestled with following God's way or my way, and most of the time it was my way. My way led me to become a teenage mother of not one, but two kids before graduating high school, failed relationships, and a multitude of hard struggles thereafter.

Being a high school student with two kids, and two different baby fathers was painful. I heard just about every stream of negative gossip and shameful, degrading, whorish, and hurtful name-calling about me that you could think of. I could hear the judging, and see the looks of contempt on people's faces when they saw me; this little five foot, one hundred and five-pound teenager carrying an infant, and pregnant with another one. Some of my friends' parents didn't want them hanging around me anymore; feeling I was a bad influence. They said I wasn't going anywhere in life, and that I had thrown my future away. Hearing those things hurt; I was shamed, embarrassed, and wanted to crawl in a hole and hide from the world. Not to mention how badly I had hurt and disappointed my parents. I didn't want to be a burden to them. I got a job, found a low-income house in the projects, and moved out, while still in high school.

I moved thirty minutes away from my parents. My home was centered in a high crime neighborhood of poverty, drugs, and dysfunction. Home invasions, substance abuse, teenage pregnancy, and murder were considered the norm. One day a swarm of police came to my house with guns and arrested my daughter's father. He was convicted of first-degree murder, and sentenced to over twenty-five years in prison. My son's father battled a serious drug addiction, and secretly moved far across the country. After several home invasions and increasing neighborhood crime, things became too dangerous, and unsafe for me and my kids. Therefore, I moved shortly after my high school graduation.

I worked full-time, went to college, accomplished several certifications, and a license in cosmetology. I worked two jobs, and went to school for many years until I graduated nursing school and became a registered nurse. This did not leave much time for God.

I was determined and worked hard to be successful to cover up the shame and guilt of being a teenage mother. Throughout the years I've carried this unexplained void and feeling of emptiness. No matter what I accomplished, how great my relationships were, or how much I was loved, that unexplained emptiness stuck with me.

In most of my relationships, the romantic love seemed to prematurely die out, which structured the thought that I was incapable of loving someone enough to marry them. Those thoughts deepened when my mother's best friend was murdered, and shortly after, my best friend was murdered by her husband. I remember telling several friends, I didn't think I could love anyone enough to marry them. Many times I cried, feeling incomplete; as if something was wrong with me. That all changed when I came across this beautiful smile that changed my life forever.

From the day we met, to the day we got married, life was like a fairytale. This man with the smile was a God-fearing, praying man. He was family-oriented, intelligent, generous, a six-figure income earner, a multi-business owner, and a minister. This minister captured my heart. Almost every date I was flourished with roses, gifts, handwritten poems, early morning prayer calls, lavish trips, walks in the park, and motorcycle rides. He was easy to love and convinced me I was his soulmate. He was like a God-sent; my real-life knight in shining armor. Feeling like I had finally found love, I didn't hesitate to say, "yes" when he asked me to marry him. We had a beautiful wedding, I was overjoyed to have married someone I loved, and was in love with.

Less than three months after we were married, it was like a nuclear bomb went off in my life. Things quickly changed for the worse. Here comes the drama, lies, mysterious phone calls, women, unexplained time loss, constant pain, repeated abuse, betrayal, ungodly behavior, and serial adultery. Almost every area of my life was being *infected*. Over thirty times, I encountered my husband engaged in extra marital affairs. My son developed a sudden episode of bipolar depression and was admitted to a crisis center. My daughter's best friend was tragically murdered. She was unable to cope with the death of her best friend, she went through cycles of depression, and couldn't provide basic needs for my grandson.

In the midst of it all, my step-father died during the Christmas holiday season. He and my mother had been married almost thirty years. As I grieved through the pain and intense emotions, I remained strong for my mom and siblings. I continued to pray and go to church; asking others to pray for us, and believing God would change things. But nothing changed. Throughout all this, I kept a smile on my face, yet I was dying on the inside.

Things were weighing in on me, and I was changing for the worse. I was angry, hurt, and shamed. I was reacting with so much anger, and emotions to the things my husband was doing, and to what I was finding out. I was fighting back and reacting just as badly as the people that hurt me. I was revengeful, my words were unfiltered ammunition, and my tongue had become more powerful than a speeding bullet.

I had suffered headaches and migraines for years, but they were coming more frequently, and lasting longer. I began having bouts of dizziness with my headaches which was unusual. I took my blood pressure and it read 214/110. I was shocked, I never had high blood pressure, and had been very active. Now my pressure was at stroke level; I was a walking time bomb! Then one day, I was taking braids out of my hair, when I noticed large patches of my natural hair coming out. The more I combed, the more hair came out. Enough hair came out to completely cover three one day old puppies. My nails were brittle, my face was breaking out, and I was always fatigued. Everything that was happening on the inside of me, was starting to be reflected outward.

I didn't like who I was, or who I was becoming. I was stressed to the max, confused, drained, and depleted with nothing left to give. Things became unsafe and dangerous between me and my husband. We eventually had to separate.

One day while I was in the shower crying, my mind was all over the place, and I was in desperate need of hearing from God. I cried out to the Lord, surrendered my all to him, and pleaded for his help. At that moment, it was as if I heard someone whisper- "Now you're ready." I began to calm down, exhausted but feeling comforted and relieved by a sudden sense of peace and transformation that was occurring.

The sense of peace and comfort that I had encountered led me to start reading my bible, attending church, and bible study, and I rejoined my old church home. I surrounded myself with people of positive spiritual influence. My family poured out so much love and support, especially my mother. Each day was getting better, I started dating myself, removing distractions, developed a thirst to know God's word, and plan for my life. Laticia Nicole's *Speaklife* prayer line and ministry also became a power source throughout my healing process.

Before I discovered I was spiritually broken, I didn't know I was broken, I thought I was good. Spiritual brokenness is why I carried feelings of incompleteness throughout many years of my life. My brokenness was a doorway for the adversary to present himself as an angel of light, and God-sent; masking his demons and his brokenness. Satan uses brokenness as a window of opportunity to enter your life, causing negative thoughts, more pain, and attaches negative spirits to your life, that can ultimately destroy you. The traumatic effects of my husband's serial malignant infidelity, brokenness, and betrayal played a significant part, and contributed to my breakdown. I had to face my grief and wrestle with all stages of it. But God's presence gave me strength and courage to walk through that dark valley that felt like death.

In the season of my marital dysfunction and transformation, I unknowingly inspired others to seek the same God that was healing me; including a woman my husband was misleading and had a relationship with. This woman said she came across a post on one of my social media pages of Laticia Nicole's Speak Life Prayer Line and Ministry. She engaged herself into the ministries, connected with Laticia, and encountered and developed a relationship with the Lord. She now has her own powerful testimony of the good Lord and his works.

We may not know why God places certain people in our lives, but we do know all things work together for the good. Most of us think it's the enemy that comes and interrupts us while we are living our so-called happy lives. It very well could be God's divine intervention. With God, sometimes renovation requires massive demolition.

I'm intentional about healing and being spiritually aligned with the Lord. As I embark on this continued journey and embrace emotional healing, I will not be afraid to love again; I *will* love again. Emotional healing is necessary and essential before I enter any future relationships. Emotional and inner healing with God allows me to reach my full potential, and live a more peaceful, and abundant life. Healing properly will keep me from carrying emotional baggage into future relationships.

I may not be where I want to be, but I'm so thankful I'm not where I used to be. Every day I wake up, I'm thankful, I praise Him, and try to be a better person in Christ than I was yesterday.

I'm not denying reality, there are areas of my life where my healing is in recovery. I am still a work in progress. Life can be hard and not always easy. I will be tempted, I will hurt someone, I will get hurt, afflicted, and tried, as long as I am alive. But God's word showed me that if I keep my faith in Him, stay connected to Him, and put on the whole armor of God, He will help me. He will deliver me, He will protect me, He will forgive me, and He will help me to forgive. I can trust God with my tomorrow because he was faithful with my yesterday.

God showed up at a time in my life when I had lost all hope, when I was in a dark place, and couldn't see any light. He showed up when I was so broken that I didn't think a shattered piece of glass like me was fixable. He made sure I knew it was his saving grace that brought me out of the spiritual infirmities.
I consider myself to be ***Beautifully Broken.***

A COMPILATION OF STORIES OF VICTORY

OUR STORIES
His Glory

SPEAKLIFE SERIES

*For everyone born of God
overcomes the world.
This is the victory that has
overcome the world,
even our faith.*

1 John 5:4

Monique Chantel Johnson

Monique Chantel Johnson

Monique Chantel Johnson is a born motivator, leader, gifted speaker, facilitator, published author and self-titled *Purpose Pusher*. Monique is a multifaceted business professional and works as a learning development manager, entrepreneur, notary, and as a certified financial counselor. A southern girl from New Orleans, Louisiana, Monique has a passion for women's empowerment, travel and living life on her own terms.

Monique's mission in life is to tear down the notion that women aren't enough just as they are. Her goals are to replace those ideas with the thought that women come fully equipped and are capable of being everything they desire to become. It's her life's desire to teach women how to carry the confidence to go after everything that they want out of life. Through her life challenges, Monique wants to teach the everyday woman how to overcome obstacles in the pursuit of success. Her intent is to share her journey with the hopes of inspiring other women to see their own beauty.

Stay connected with Monique:
For more information on Women's Retreats, Purpose Driven Motivation Projects, Author Events and *The Push to Purpose* and appearances by going to www.purposedrivenmotivation.com

The Road To Recovery-
Identifying a Life of Depression

I can't think of the exact moment in time that depression set in, I can only recall it hitting me like a ton of bricks. I had to be in my late teens, early twenties, when I realized that I was sad far too often. By then, I had my fair share of life woes and would later tack on being a teen mom, married at the ripe age of nineteen, and never feeling like I was enough. The secret life I lived through the depression, anger, anxiety, and resentment would later carry on well into my late thirties. At that point, I had undergone and accepted eighteen years of marital infidelity and struggled with unresolved daddy issues. I never realized that the absence of a father would spark so many life concerns. Healing from these family dynamics are challenging and can replay itself in our adult years. The pain we bear can show up in many forms: fearing to love, lack of boundaries, seeking unhealthy relationships, trust issues, feeling unworthy, starving for affection, and falling for someone's potential. The act of marital betrayal creates feelings of hopelessness, stress, anxiety, and impacts our ability to express our thoughts and regulate our emotions. Both marital infidelity and daddy issues can promote depressive behaviors creating further feelings of loneliness, fear, and distrust.

I couldn't be happy long enough to heal because trauma became cyclical. I began thinking that I was somehow predestined for pain. As healing would occur, something would tear the bandaid away from the wound, ripping the very scab away. The hurt, pain, and sadness never made room for full healing to take place; it only made room for depression to become present. This depressive behavior led to regular seasons of resentment and anger. It kept me from connecting with people and always seeing the worst in everyone I would encounter. If a grievance occurred, I would harbor those emotions for years, never allowing the anger and rage to dissipate. These responses were not intentional and usually arose because of differences in understanding, but my responses led to family fractures, disagreements, and estrangements.

Coping with depression was a feat in itself, causing various reactions; periodically ranging from somatic problems like headaches, fatigue, loss of appetite to cognitive issues like anger, guilt, fear, confusion, and social withdrawal. When people see you, they don't often see your pain. They see only what you present to the world, and that's usually a brave face with a big smile. I concealed depression like I was hiding my favorite snack. The only assumption to be made was that life was treating me relatively fair, or presumably perfect, because I lived a life of pretending- *all is well.*

In the early stages of my illness, I hid behind my feelings due to my immense sense of embarrassment. I had all of these unexplained internal emotions and could never figure out what triggered them. Instead, l lived with the compounded fear that someone would think of me as flawed, lesser, inferior, or ill, so I continued to mask my internal pains. Sadly, family bias about this illness, prevented me from sharing my secret; I feared not being viewed as being strong enough. If I expressed my feelings, I could be perceived as being weak. So I carried on week after week, month after month, year after year; pretending. I went to church, all made-up, said my Amens, fellowshipped with friends, smiled with family; all while being emotionally wounded.

I see this as a prominent issue in black families. The cultural taboos and stigma associated with depression make it difficult for any person to admit to having a problem or seeking treatment. What becomes clear is that culture and social contexts, while not the only determinants, shape how minorities seek mental treatment. Someone who's never suffered depression may have a hard time understanding or sympathizing. When people don't understand your emotional state, they use comparisons to disqualify your pain. I've been told that others have gone through worse or that my trials weren't as significant as I imagined. The comparisons reflect a discredit of one's feelings; consequentially causing emotional devastation, producing an inability to grieve.

I propose that increased awareness concerning depression could promote change in how our society reacts to mental illness. This awareness has the power to turn our community and culture away from inflicting further pain, and closer to showing love, hope, and support for those suffering. I often hear people using terms such as unhinged, psychotic, cray-cray, nuts, psycho, crazy, and making hurtful jokes. Families compare depression to having a poor family background. This thought generally limits the communication between family members, stifling the ability to vocalize evident problems. So what do families do, they turn a blind eye, ignore the issue, or tell people to pray the problems away. Those are not the only answers. Acceptance does not equal spiritual failure or that depression, anxiety, or another disorder is your identity; it means that it is a condition affecting your life. It's time to change the narrative by showing love, empathy, and compassion. We have to learn how to show support in helping those dealing with depression seek help if required.

Seeking Help

An adverse circumstance didn't always trigger my depression. However, it still crept into my life like a thief in the night; stealing yet another little piece of me. The final bout of depression lingered on longer than any time before. I was forced to seek treatment because this time, it brought along a little friend named anxiety. I woke up one morning, unable to face the world. I pulled the duvet over my head and willed yet another day away. I couldn't shake the roving thoughts. They overpowered me, taking me through a dark tunnel of fears and self-loathing. The heart palpitations, sweaty hands, unconscionable feelings, lack of motivation, sadness, and the toxic mixture of both depression and anxiety had gotten the better of me. After day three, I would peel my body from the bed and contact the behavioral help clinic at my local military base hospital. Every step I took in efforts to get dressed for this appointment felt like I was just dragging my body through water. I had to force myself to shower, comb my hair, and of course, put on a little makeup. No need to also *look* depressed, right? Masking my condition had become the norm. I had grown accustomed to *putting lipstick on a pig* by presenting an image of being well to keep my inner darkness in check.

Before making it to the hospital, everything that could go wrong did. When you are in despair, these emotions are heightened. Before leaving the house, every fire alarm goes off. I would then run frantically throughout the house to ensure there wasn't a present fire. When all was clear, I jumped into the car with only minutes to spare. As I'm entering the Air Force base, I almost get into a vehicle collision. I had previously been involved in a terrible car accident that left me with a sudden case of Post-Traumatic Stress Disorder and internal scars I still bear. When I finally made it, I signed into the hospital front desk to be seen, although ten minutes late. My name is called, and I'm greeted by a tall gentleman who ignored my very existence. As we walked down this long hallway, I trudged along maybe two to three feet behind him. We would make our way in this cold, dark room with only a lamp to illuminate the space. Minutes go by as he typed on his computer, still not saying a word and never making eye contact. He then mumbles the words- "You've been properly checked in, and your doctor is on the way." I finally made my way into the room with my now physician to bear my heart. I'm angry, sad, depressed, and full of rage. I would go on to state that my experience was subpar, and she wasn't the least bit concerned about it.

As the appointment with my physician concluded, she offered me nothing more than a recommendation for a future appointment, a homework assignment, and the option to download a few phone applications meant for coping. I believed that there had to be another way. A way to cope, a way to heal, a way to get out of the state of depression. It was time that I sought help from the only source I knew that had healed me in the past - God! I had gone to the mat for everything else except this. I've overcome many hardships. However, I failed to seek the Father because I thought I had this under control. There was real work to be done, and prayer was a significant addition to my plan for my healing. It's easy to lose faith when pain is plaguing the mind, body, and spirit. But it's never too late to begin bettering yourself and pushing past the pain. A constant reminder was Isaiah 41:10, NIV- *So do not fear, for I am with*

*you; do not be dismayed, for I am your God. I will strengthen you and help you;
I will uphold you with my righteous right hand.*

The Breakthrough

Returning home from that appointment was the actual turning point of my life. It took many days of prayer, and several visits to a counselor before life would change. But, when I look back over my life, I realize that God was with me every step of the way. The first step to healing was accepting that there was an issue, which required that I face my problems head-on. That meant healing from an abusive marriage. Through prayer, marital counseling, boundary clarification, and putting in the much-needed work, we remain a couple of twenty-three years. I don't want to mislead you in thinking this was easy. In fact, it was challenging, but we've persevered. I also had to come to grips with my daddy issues. My father and I have had a successful relationship now for more than twenty years. However, when I attempted to seek closure from the past, I was met with lies, excuses, and deception. I guess I could have become bitter and resentful, but I refused to allow it to taint my spirit. It was apparent that my father will never accept accountability for his actions. I had to forgive him despite the apology, I may never receive.

The question I'm frequently asked is whether I'm still depressed, and the answer is not today. Truthfully, I have learned how to cope, and I no longer hide behind my feelings. I am not ashamed of who I was and who I've become. There is power in your struggle, but you have to be willing to stand up to your mountains and have the desire to seek help when necessary. I am living proof that you can survive depression and anxiety.

There are practical steps you can take to heal on your road to recovery:

1. Retrain your brain to respond appropriately to the non-emergencies of everyday life, all while working to deal with old traumas.

2. Pray, especially when negative emotions are flared. Prayer changes things.

3. Acknowledge the pain by being intentional and recognizing what hurts.

4. You may never forget, but FORGIVE! Forgiveness is a necessary part of healing. Not just forgiveness of people, but forgiveness of yourself! You have to let go of the pain.

5. Seek counseling if required! Disregard the naysayers and family stigmas. Your mental health is important. Don't allow the rampant prejudice of seeking help to discourage you from doing what is best.

6. Love yourself! You can't have love for others without truly loving yourself.

7. Set healthy boundaries by tuning into your feelings and discontinue doing anything that takes away from your happiness.

8. Practice self-awareness! If you notice yourself slipping into old habits, make a conscious effort to make changes immediately.

9. Protect your peace! John 14:27, KJV- *Peace I leave with you; my peace I give unto you: not as the world giveth, give I unto to you. Let not your heart be troubled, neither let it be afraid.*

10. Have self-compassion! You are not, and will never be perfect. Give yourself some grace when things go awry and note that those moments are only temporary.

The Power of Prayer and Overcoming

The things I've experienced were emotional sources of pain, but weren't my identity. Depression, anxiety, and other similar challenges are not signs of God's absence; they are the toils of this life. Christ is in you and not distant from your life battles. Depression is an attack from the enemy of the mind. Living with depression is a mind under siege, and we need to stay alert and motivated so that the enemy doesn't attempt to destroy our lives. Deuteronomy 31:8, NIV- *The Lord himself goes before you and will be with you;* **he will never leave you nor forsake you.** *Do not be afraid; do not be discouraged.*

I'd like to comfort you, my friend, that if you've ever experienced any of what I've been through, I see you. I am you. I want you to know that you are not alone in your battles. You can change your life by standing tall in your power. God's grace is sufficient for every part of life that feels like a thorn. We are complete in him, and rest assured, he has already made us whole. Because of the many strengths that both women and men possess, we can overcome and recover from most obstacles by merely praying and believing in ourselves.

Men, you are our kings; you are strong and full of valor. You represent gallant bravery and strength. You are overcomers! Women, you are magical and powerful! You are life's nurturers. Because of your strength, you can bear the burdens of the world, all while supporting your family and community. You are overcomers! On this rocky road of life, I pray that it leads you to healing and recovery! May the lord continue to guide your way!

A COMPILATION OF STORIES OF VICTORY

OUR STORIES
His Glory

SPEAKLIFE SERIES

But thanks be to God! He gives us the victory through our Lord Jesus Christ.

1 Corinthians 15:57

Pamela Thompson Smith

Pamela Thompson Smith

Pamela Thompson Smith resides in Raleigh, North Carolina. She is an entrepreneur at heart. She is owner of Thompson Smith Consulting, a full service consulting firm specializing in non- profit fundraising and development, special event planning and coordination, corporate events, marketing, public relations, and community outreach.

She graduated in 1991 with a Bachelor of Arts Degree in Radio, Television and Motion Pictures from the University of North Carolina at Chapel Hill.

With a passion for events and promotions, Pamela managed the Promotions Departments for Radio Stations FOXY 107/104 in Raleigh North Carolina for several years.

Her love for marketing led her into restaurant advertising and marketing in 2000 and she worked for over 15 years from home and traveled extensively as a Field Marketing Business Consultant for Pizza Hut, Taco Bell, Sonic Drive-in and Rita's Italian Ice Restaurant Chains where she facilitated local store marketing, promotional and operational strategies in North Carolina, South Carolina, Virginia, West Virginia, Maryland, and Florida.

In 2015, Pamela became a full-time entrepreneur. She has served as corporate planner for Capitol Broadcasting Company's FOX Family Fun Fest, Development Manager for Raleigh Executive Luncheon for NC Med Assist, and as Donor and Special Events Contractor for Clinton College.

In addition to Event Planning, Pam found her niche in non-profit development and fundraising. She has served for seven years as the Event Planner and Development Coordinator for the Triangle Martin Luther King Committee, Inc. for the execution of the MLK Holiday Celebration Events. She has also served as Non-Profit Fundraising Consultant for Clinton College, Rock Hill, South Carolina, NC Med Assist, Charlotte, North Carolina, African American Cultural Festival, Raleigh, North Carolina, and other non-profits.

She was recently named Interim Executive Director for the non-profit African American Cultural Festival where she will guide the overall vision and coordination of programs and operations to successfully plan, program and present the 2020 African American Cultural Festival.

.

One of her favorite quotes is **when work is what you love to do, it is not work- it is SERVING!** She loves her work and is THANKFUL for every opportunity to serve. She continues to serve many clients across the Triangle and other areas in many roles. It is her PASSION that makes the difference.

She is the radio host for The Community Impact segment which airs monthly on the Sports Shop Radio Show, a WRAL Station and co-host of The Art of Balancing It All Podcast which airs on Podbean, ITunes, Spotify, and Google Podcast.

Pam is the 2016 winner of the ACHI Magazine Woman of Achievement Award and 2015 Martin Luther King Humanitarian Award.

Pam is an inspirational emcee, speaker, and praise and worship leader. She truly loves the Lord with all her heart and is always willing to serve. She is a member of Centennial AME Zion Church which is in her hometown of Bear Creek, North Carolina where she has served as Preacher Steward for over 27 years.

She wears many hats, stands daily on the promises of Jeremiah 29:11, serves in many roles; and her proudest role is that of Mom to her daughter who is currently a sophomore at Louisburg College, Louisburg, North Carolina.

Faking It INSTEAD OF *Faith-In It*
Dedicated in memory of my Uncle Lewis Thompson

O ur Stories, HIS Glory has allowed me to reflect upon times in my life when I was driven by a need to please people instead of being driven by my God, my faith, and my deepest desires. I titled this time in my life as a period of faking it instead of faith-in it. It wasn't until I started faith-in it that I was able to recognize God's true Glory as it fell upon my life. I can tell you about a girl who had an amazing childhood, full of love and rooted in faith in God; a girl who knew what she wanted her life to look like. I have always been a communicator; a social butterfly with a desire to shine in every area of my life. I was taught and believed that no one could stop me because I could do all things through Christ. However, there was a period of time when I let what others thought paralyze my growth in many ways.

I remember my high school guidance counselor recommended that instead of just applying to my one and only choice for college, which was the University of North Carolina at Chapel Hill, with a Major in Broadcasting, that I should look at Historically Black Colleges and Universities. There was nothing wrong with those awesome choices, but I wanted to be a Tar Heel! I did the work and God's Glory fell upon me when I only applied to one college, UNC-CH and was accepted! My story, HIS Glory!!!

I have always been a planner at heart, so my life was planned out for the next several years...I received my degree, worked in the radio industry and found my passion for events and marketing, a good man found me, and we married. I was starting a great career and everything seemed fine, but something wasn't right. The years went by as I just went through the motions. Then one day, seven years into my marriage, I witnessed a miracle. God's most precious blessing in the form of a baby girl after a traumatic

---

81

and dangerous pregnancy! I was told for years it would be unlikely that I could carry a child to full term. My Story, His Glory! I forgot about any issues and became distracted by the new love in our life; our miracle baby girl. It was all about her! Being a full time Mom triggered within me a desire to start my own business. Soon I was motivating and inspiring a team of 50 women daily as a Mary Kay Sales Director. I was so busy listening to the *noise,* building that presentation for the world to see that I didn't fix what was broken in me and in my marriage. I didn't dare share that there were problems, I convinced myself that we were alright and we coasted until year thirteen. I worried about what it looked like for me to love and trust God, and still have a failed marriage. Why not stay? I had a husband, my adorable child, a new job working from home, the nice house, the cars; I seemed to have it all from the outside looking in. My presentation was great. Surely this is where God wanted for me. Sometimes smiles are learned behavior to mask the unhappiness inside. People only show you what they want you to see. My grandmother taught us to always pray. I began to pray more, over everything concerning my life.

The outside looked picture- perfect, but really nothing had changed on the inside for me. The song says- "in the midnight hour God is going to turn it around." Well, in the midnight hour God took me to my funeral. I could see all my family and friends gathered, sharing stories of how wonderful, kind, motivating and inspiring I had been. The tributes were just as I expected, because that's what I do. I help others to carry their cross and oftentimes, I never let them know when I am leaning because my own cross is too heavy to bear. Never asking for help; I was afraid to be transparent. In my midnight dream, one woman said- "she was just one of the happiest people I know." I was standing back, somewhere in the crowd, yelling out- "that wasn't me, I am the one broken, no I am the one UNHAPPY, no, that wasn't me!" No one could hear me or even notice me. I woke up crying out to God; literary shaking and crying. Something changed at that very moment.... I changed my prayer. I knew if something didn't change that would be my story. The dream shocked me into my true reality. My Story, His Glory!

That night I changed my prayer, and I asked- "God, please cover my family and God, please change my story, and give me long life." I wanted God to do a new thing in me and for me. I was tired of going through the motions, and I no longer wanted to just exist; I wanted to live my best life, and not for people but by His design. I wanted and needed more. I knew God still had great plans for me. So I began to ask God, every day to change my story, I didn't pray for the things I wanted, I didn't pray for the things I needed, which is what we tend to do. Those things may not even line up with His will for our lives. I simply prayed for God to cover my family and change my story and give me long life. He didn't come quickly, but He's always on time. Two years later, God gave me the clarity, courage, strength and the resources to act out a new story. I packed up without telling anyone, once again afraid of judgement, and started a new story, featuring now just me and my daughter. Then a year later after sixteen years of marriage, I found myself, a 41-year old divorced, single mommy; yet at peace in a new chapter filled with mixed emotions. There is a quote from a book I read during this emotional time that posed the question- *"have you ever been in the worst of times and the best of times at the same time?"* That was me. I hated the fall out of my decision, but I was so proud of myself for finally being courageous enough to trust God for better days. However, because I was so intentional in my presentation of the happy life, as I helped and encouraged others to do, my decision to divorce looked crazy to others. When you stop faking it and faith-in it people won't always understand the vision God gave you. But you have to trust God, not people. It's not their fault, they are going off the painting you drew of your life. The steps that I was taking to get my joy, my peace, and have the best life for me and my daughter was painful but necessary. My Story, His Glory.

God began to move mightily in my life. He was changing my story. I began a new career that took me all around the United States weekly. I also owned my own business; the money was good and I was able to provide well for my daughter and myself. A new story was being written, chapter after chapter filled with highs and lows and bounce back testimonies of His goodness toward me. Once again I was intentional in making it look like, from the outside looking in, that the pieces that were broken were magically put back together by a choice I made without the work. I never did the work to fix what was broken, I am not sure at this point if I even took the time to dive into what caused the brokenness. I just moved on and became busy crafting another presentation of *noise* that I presented to the world in my new story. I failed to do the work to heal and get over people, and the mistakes of the previous story. My Story, His Glory.

In 2011, on my birthday, I was one, in a group of employees who were laid off; I lost a very high paying job. What was I going to do? Still caught up in that presentation for others, only the people closest to me knew what was going on. I started my part-time event planning business, and I continued intentionally to not look like what I was going through. I focused on keeping the right perspective, I looked like a million bucks; my hair was laid, my clothes were sharp, and I always had a praise on my lips. If a woman can make herself look good, she feels good, even when she silently shoulders the weight of the world. I posted positive things every morning on Facebook. Then after taking my daughter to school and returning home, I sometimes found myself curled up on the couch in tears, in a fetal position for hours at a time. I continued to encourage everyone, while holding back on being transparent; revealing the part that gave God Glory and not revealing the part that showed my flaws, insecurities, struggles, hardships and desperation. I would tell you God made a way, but never tell you about the days before the way was made. People look for your faith in how you move in your darkest times….do you still trust God, are you still speaking affirmations of encouragement when you can't trace God in your situation. My words and my praise never wavered no matter the circumstance. So, where is the contradiction you ask…. God couldn't use me and my storm for his Glory and show people how he can bring you out if I was afraid to be transparent and tell the whole story. Instead I focused on always looking like the pieces were perfectly put together; faking it instead of faith in it. My Story, His Glory.

After sixteen months I received a new job that still enabled me to work from home and afforded me the flexibility and the ability to travel throughout the United States. This time He knew that I needed a flexible schedule. He was already putting things in place that would enable me to positively respond to situations that would come later. In 2013 my Mom was diagnosed with breast cancer. With the flexibility of my new job, I was able to drop off and pick up my daughter from school and never miss a weekly chemo treatment with my Mom. I would often leave her chemo treatments tired mentally and physically, and get back on the road to head to the next city, praying that His healing power was manifesting over my Mom's body with each treatment because I couldn't imagine life without her. A year later my Mom was completely healed from cancer! My Story, His Glory.

Fast forward to a few years ago, now divorced over ten years, a single Mom, with an active high school teenager, God showed me in another dream that it was time to come off the road. I knew Him as our provider and trusted him. So I decided to leave my great job to take another job that allowed me to work from home with no travel, but a lot less money. I continued to also work my event planning company part-time. This was my passion and I delighted in every opportunity to plan an event. Nine months later I found myself unemployed once again, and unsure where to turn. Yet, I knew God as a promise keeper. I was determined not to be capsized by the storms of life, but determined to make it through. God's direction was taking me somewhere where I had to learn to bend to the waves of the storm and not break. The remnants of the debris in my life from my storms left me sometimes feeling helpless, hopeless, defeated, and unworthy and questioning *why,* but continuing to pray and ask God that same prayer- "God, change my story and give me long life," He guided me through one storm after another storm; always bringing me out victorious. My ship had set sail years prior when I decided to step out in the deep; tired of going through the motions, stepping out in an effort to live a better life and be true to myself based on my choices. God allowed the storms to rage in my life, but each storm was rocking my ship and guiding me in His desired direction. Like Paul in the bible, I knew Jesus was riding in the storm with me, and in my darkest hours, when it looked like the ship was going down, like Paul I stood on his promises to me. I declared I might lose everything, but there will be no loss of life. I will not die. I will make it to shore even if I have to float on the broken pieces. (Acts 27: 21-25) and over the years by faith everything that felt like a disaster turned into my miracle. I know God as a restorer. He will give you double for your trouble, and restore more than what you think you lost. My Story, His Glory. But I never told the full story.

Truth opens the door for total transformation. My success, my victories, my work load, my business, my disappointments, my heart breaks, all the noise and the motion allowed me to hide and not heal. I recently experienced watching my beloved uncle die with me alone in the room. For hours I listened to what appeared to be what they call a loud death rattle. I dozed off, but subconsciously was still listening for the rattle which was a sign that he was still breathing. When there was no noise, no rattle, I was awakened out of my sleep because of the silence. My uncle had taken his last breath. No one was there in that silence but me and God and He used that moment to speak loudly to me. It was in that moment of silence that healing took place for my uncle, no more sickness, and no more troubles of this world. God reminded me that it is in that same stillness and silence that my healing can take place. That I have been hiding in the loud *noise* and couldn't clearly hear Him but that silence in that moment is the loudest noise I will ever hear. It's time to hear Him; to be intentional about slowing down and getting to a place daily where I can seek His face and hear his voice. In this new found stillness I shall find refuge, deliverance, healing and direction for all He has for me. I hear God saying to me that- *The great things that I have for you and your purpose are not in the noise you are listening for. Be still and know I am GOD, and you shall hear my voice and I will deliver you and guide you.* My story changed yet again, at that moment, when the silence became the loudest noise I will ever hear.

My Story.... His Glory!

A COMPILATION OF STORIES OF VICTORY

OUR STORIES
His Glory

SPEAKLIFE SERIES

But thanks be to God! He gives us the victory through our Lord Jesus Christ.

1 Corinthians 15:57

Samantha Huntley

Samantha Huntley

Trendsetter, Educator, Beauty Columnist, Salon Owner, and Celebrity Master Hairstylist are all titles for Samantha Huntley. Samantha served as the Educational and Artistic Director for Bronner Brothers Professional Sales Division from 2003-2014. Although it is extremely rare for one individual to hold both positions, the dynamic Durham, North Carolina native's stellar background declares she was well equipped to handle the job. Part of her unique responsibilities were to ensure that educators under her tutelage had a strong understanding of the ingredients in all Bronner Brothers Professional Sales products how these ingredients not only contribute to haircare but also the execution of the hottest techniques that yield a plethora of exciting runway-worthy looks. Huntley's flawless finishes have grace the pages in publications throughout the United States, the Caribbean, Tokyo, and London. Samantha has won numerous awards in categories such as, Fantasy, Braids, and Total Look. As the Artistic Educational Director, Samantha was heavily immersed in the professional Sales production for the Bronner Brothers International Beauty Show. She was responsible for selecting the educators, models, makeup artist, talent, and the lighting and props for the stage as well as the overall theme for the show. With all of these responsibilities on her slim shoulders Samantha, as salon owner, still managed to successfully service her Durham based clientele.

Currently, Samantha showcasing her "behind-the-scenes " talent locally, styling hair for music videos, and campaigns and producing fashion shows. Samantha is also celebrating two years of successful service as the ultimate Image Consultant; helping men and women cultivate the image of their dreams with Body Contouring, Scalp Micropigmentation, Hair Replacement, Hair Styling and Wardrobe Styling. Samantha is passionate about everything pertaining to beauty and she is very happy to add another acclaimed title to her list of accomplishments- Author..

Welcome Mat

Deion Sanders once said, "If you look good, you feel good. If you feel good, you play good. If you play good, they pay good." As a hairstylist, I know this to be true—from my own feelings after getting dolled up and from my clients' reactions after looking in the mirror. It's true: You do your best when you feel your best. And helping women look and feel their best is my life's purpose. It's what I've wanted to do since I was a little girl. Add in my entrepreneurial spirit and that equaled owning and operating a hair salon.

My dream came true when I stopped renting booths and opened my own salon in 1999. Then, as dreams do, it evolved. I no longer just wanted to be behind the chair. I wanted my name to be known, to learn more and to be a bigger force in the industry. So I sought out opportunities to make it happen and landed the perfect job with an internationally acclaimed hair and skincare manufacturer. It was a stellar brand with a stellar reputation.

I worked really hard and within three years, I gained two director positions—the Artistic and Educational Director. It's usually a different person holding each title. First, I was appointed the Artistic Director position. Then when the initial Educational Director left, I was asked if I wanted the job. I figured I wasn't lazy and I could read, and learn, so I decided to take on the challenge. And to say it was a challenge would be an understatement. There was no roadmap, no blueprint, no book of standard operating procedures. Nothing. Whatever the last director did, he took with him. I had to figure it out as I went along.

It was very stressful; yet, it was also exciting. Wherever the company had sales territory, we needed a sales ambassador present to secure relationships. My job was to train our trainers and make sure they had the materials they needed to go into any sales territory and educate stylists on our brand and how to use our products. So I was flown to many exciting places such as New York, Miami, Texas and places as far as the Caribbean and London, England.

Taking on the two positions, I did everything from employing people, to formatting our educational seminars. We also had two International Beauty Shows every year and I did everything for the Professional Sales Division; selecting lighting, approving the set design, selecting the educators, the wardrobe designer, the models, the runway coach, the music and the lighting. If a hair appliance company wanted to be contracted, they had to come through me, because I would have to approve the product and train my staff. I was the go-to girl. Because the company was so well-known, over the course of my 15 years with them, my name also, elevated pretty high in popularity. When I walked into nightclubs, people sought me out because they knew I was casting for an upcoming show.

I was also in charge of ad campaigns for magazines, so I was always able to say- "my work has been published." I could get photographers and makeup artists to work for free or little to nothing. Note: I wasn't trying to get over on people at all. I'm a strong believer in paying people what they're worth. However, when I started with that particular division of the company, it was about 15 years old, so everything I did was under a very tight budget. If you've ever had to make do with little resources, personally or professionally, you know how valuable that skill is. Year after year, from about 2003 until 2014, I made miracles happen with very tight budgets.

All the while, I still ran my salon back in North Carolina. And my clients were proud to say their stylist was teaching in London or Miami, or wherever in the world I'd be. People are attracted to movers and shakers, and I could back it up. I could open up the latest issues of Upscale Magazine and show that I had been published. So although my schedule was tight, the salon stayed full. If I only worked the salon two days out of the week, my hands and feet were busy from the time I opened the door at five in the morning until I closed over fifteen hours later.

The problem was: I wasn't nourishing *my baby*. The business stayed open, but I did nothing to ensure its growth. I wasn't bringing in new stylists or promoting the business. I'd gotten so caught up in the privilege and prestige of representing such a stellar company, that I let my own dream fall by the wayside. An even bigger problem than that, was the fact that I didn't even realize that I was neglecting my business until my division went under new management. The new Vice President of Professional Sales, my new supervisor, walked into my salon one day and fired me.

I was his direct line of communication; there was no one in between us. Because he was new to the position, I felt he should have communicated with me about the role the educational team and I contributed to the international trade shows. "How are things going for the show? What's your strategy to promote and generate sales?" Those are questions he could have used to start the conversation. "What's to come under your reign?", I wondered. "What's next?" I got no information, so whatever his plans were, I knew I wasn't a part of them. However, I remained hopeful.

I'll never forget the day he walked into my plush downtown beauty salon. He took a seat, made himself comfortable and proceeded to loudly exclaim to me and the entire salon that my position had been terminated. I paused, blinked my eyes, then put on my game face.

"The six-hour journey you made to tell me that wasn't necessary," I said.

He stood up and said, "I'm no punk," then added, "Perhaps we can work together in the future."

I laughed, thanked him for the invitation, and shook my head. "No, thank you."

I knew he was coming, so I kept my schedule light that day. Although I knew what he was coming for, it was still a rude awakening. I walked out of my salon, got in my car and sat there for like an hour. I couldn't even leave the parking lot. "What now?" I wondered. I was like a fish out of water. Not only had I lost a significant source of income, but I felt like I had lost my identity. After all, I gave my company fifteen years of my life.

For a long time, it felt like the world had ended. I didn't have the luxury of staying in that feeling. I didn't have a husband to hold me down until I got it together. I had bills at home and at my salon to pay. So I packed my feelings up and dove headfirst back into my business. My mistake was loud and clear though: I got too caught up in trying to wear as many hats as I could, trying to make myself as valuable and sustainable as possible, to lock my position in. All the while, I was doing my own business a disservice.

My business had long since stopped being my priority. Consequently, over the course of those 15 years, I stopped making time for my own entrepreneurial endeavors. I could've made time, though. As Artistic and Educational Director, I had two assistants. I could've delegated many of my responsibilities to them, but I chose not to, out of fear. I figured because no one had taught me the ropes when I took the job, I essentially didn't want to teach anyone how to replace me. They'd ask how they could help and I'd redirect them to their responsibilities as educators. As far as helping me prepare; I refused help. I never mistreated them, but I intentionally handled the logistics on my own.

Another disservice was to my personal relationships; so much so that my fiancé walked in the bathroom one day and told me he didn't want me anymore. I was *devastated*. I cried my heart out then brushed myself off and kept going. I snuggled all my eggs in my one basket as an Artistic and Educational director for a multi-million-dollar company that flew me all over the world to do what I loved. I don't even think I gave myself time to process it and heal. I just kept it moving and took it in stride.

I don't regret my personal relationship ending because it was damaged on both sides beyond repair. However, I didn't leave when I knew I should have. I rolled my eyes at his wrongdoings and kept my head in the game. We paid bills together which worked for my wallet. My productivity was my priority. I know the relationship ending so abruptly still bothered me, because about four months after I moved out, he called to wish me a happy birthday. I was in Florida at the time. I thought I was over him; yet, that call triggered another breakdown about the failed relationship.

The pain and hardship from my professional separation took a similar, though more drastic toll, on me. It took *years* to recover from that heartbreak. Yeah, I picked up the pieces and kept moving, but I was still hurt. I started doing things like Groupon to replace the monetary side of the business that I'd lost with my termination. I also started doing more freelance work, including becoming the beauty editor for a local magazine. That kept me doing my photoshoots, spreading knowledge about the industry, and kept my salon visible. I started doing more local fashion shows and teamed up with promoters when they were hosting events.

There were disadvantages at every turn. As the Artistic Director for an Internationally-known company, I had the best photographers and makeup artists at my fingertips. Exposure was a huge selling point for such a major brand. I was constantly selling dreams. When I was no longer wearing that hat, I lost all of those connections. I no longer had a dream to sell. And it took a long time to build a rolodex of good artists to partner with as a small business owner.

Thankfully that happened before I started consulting, which is something that I really enjoy. As the Artistic Director I was in charge of ad campaigns, research and development on products, and descriptions on how to use products. I remember feeling slightly incompetent because writing was never my strongpoint. However, I rolled my sleeves up and figured it out. I remembered what a writing teacher told me once: "You have to make them see a picture. You have to make them see what you're talking about." So it would take me a whole day to do one of the course descriptions, because I had to use the right words and make the people want to come to our events. I was competing with other manufacturers and my only tools were the words and a picture. So I got plenty of practice.

That practice paid off once I started consulting. I finally reached the light at the end of a long tunnel. For about six years, I struggled with reclaiming and maybe even redesigning my identity as a woman, as an artist, and as a business owner. I'm beginning to breathe easy and know I'm good enough on my own; I don't need that company name attached to me anymore to be great. I can finally answer the *what now* question, and my answer is simple: Do what you've always loved doing, but with the knowledge that you've since gained. The title may no longer be mine, but the skills I acquired belong to me forever.

Every area of my business is growing. I love teaching, so I'm a consultant for startup haircare brands. I love making women look and feel good, so in addition to doing wigs for cancer patients and survivors, I also offer treatments such as non-invasive body contouring and scalp micropigmentation, which is a nonsurgical hair restoration technique. I restore dignity to people who are in crises. If you lose your hair, for many people that's like losing a limb. Sometimes it's from cancer. Other times it's from bad maintenance or improper techniques, or it can be hereditary or stress-related.

Witnessing the transformation in someone's spirit when they come in, especially the hair loss clients, never gets old. It's not just my skills, but my bedside manner. This is my life's calling, to help people in more ways than just the exterior. When you lose your hair, you feel bad. Some people take it in stride but most don't. They really have challenges and when you see them smiling and saying, "Oh my God, my husband is going to love this" or "my children are going to love it," you know you've done your job. They feel beautiful and for me, making someone feel beautiful is one of the best feelings in the world.

I received numerous awards for the director positions and my artistic ability. I'm an award-winning stylist, I'm a beauty editor, and I am most proud of being a hair restoration specialist. I'm also a home-owner again. I didn't let my situation with my ex-fiancé stop me. Home ownership is something that I wanted for myself, so I earned it.

Happy endings aren't stumbled upon; they're earned. Something devastating happened to me and I could've shrunk behind the disappointment and disappeared, but I didn't. Turns out, it was the best thing that ever happened to me. It was time to go. There was nothing more for me to learn. I'd done everything. Had I been monitoring or doing a better job of taking care of my brand, I may have left on my own before I was terminated.

When you're using Corporate America to hold things down for you while you pursue your dreams, don't forget that it's a vessel to get you to the promised land. Don't neglect your corner store because you're managing the meat department in somebody else's supermarket—regardless how much privilege and prestige it comes with. Make sure that all the skills and talents you're using for that company, you're using for yourself as well.

It's okay to hurt and cry for a while, but don't stay there. You have to pick yourself back up. Figure out where you went wrong, cry it out, then stand up. Remember the calling over your life. Remember that something very disappointing can actually be something really beneficial for you. Remember to **sweep your welcome mat.** Remember that your future and your joy is your responsibility.

A COMPILATION OF STORIES OF VICTORY

OUR STORIES
His Glory

SPEAKLIFE SERIES

May we shout for joy over your victory and lift up our banners in the name of our God. May the LORD grant all your requests.

Psalm 20:5

Samantha Williams

Samantha Williams

Samantha Williams has 15 years of experience in the cleaning industry. She has worked at prestigious companies where she has learned the ins and outs of the business. She is passionate about providing the best services to her clients, as she is a very detailed and organized individual. Samantha decided to become an entrepreneur; she is part owner of a cleaning business and has implemented and perfected her own skill set to reach clientele across the Raleigh-Durham, North Carolina area. She also is an independent travel agent, working for a well-known travel company.

Contact Samantha:
Email: williamss0709@gmail.com
Myvortex365.com/SWtravels Surge365.com/SWtravels
Facebook: @SamanthaWilliams

Don't Allow Grief to Consume You

H ave you ever thought that someone would live forever? Well, in my case I most definitely thought that all my family would live forever. I didn't think I would have to figure out how to go through life without them.

My childhood was amazing! Growing up, it was always me and mom. She had me at the age of 16, while she was still in high school. Even though she was young, she was so determined to create a good life for the two of us. After my birth, my mom continued her studies and graduated with her high school diploma. With the help of her family, my mom furthered her education, and secured employment in the corporate world, where she experienced success for many years. She was a highly motivated woman; she always wanted me to experience the many things she didn't get the opportunity to do during her childhood and teen-age years. Some years it wasn't easy for us, but my mom made sure I never wanted for anything. She made sure that I was able to be involved in many extracurricular activities, and we were always traveling somewhere. We enjoyed each other to the fullest, and had great times together.

When they were growing up, my mom had a great relationship with her sister. I could tell that my mom's go- to person for any and everything had been her sister; they had a special bond. When I came along, my aunt became like a second mother to me; the three of us were very close. Over time, the bond between my aunt and me was just as strong as the bond between my mom and my aunt. It might have been even stronger because my aunt and I spent so much time together.

Growing up, I was a church girl; my aunt stayed in church. I can remember feeling like I went to church seven days a week! Even then, I knew God was real. I got saved at the age of seven. I didn't really understand, but I knew that God did great things for the people around me in the church, and I wanted that same feeling. I loved praise and worship, and as I got older, I fell in love with praise dancing and my mother loved to see me dance. I loved seeing the beautiful smile on her face, as she sat in that audience, and hearing her loudly screaming- "That's my baby!" It was the best feeling ever.

Fast forward to my senior year in high school. Mom and I were so excited that I was graduating; Mom would tear up talking about how happy we were. She also would say that when I graduated, she and my aunt were going on a cruise, and they wouldn't be able to be reached for a few days! Truly it was a dream come true that I was going to walk the stage. During my senior year I went on the high school choir trip to Washington D.C. My mom was so nervous for me to go, and so was I because I was never really allowed to stay anywhere but at my aunt's house and grandmother's house. So, this was my first big out-of-town trip without my mom. I called her every day, all throughout the day, just to check in, and it made her day! Until..... that one day when there was no answer. I called and called and called, and still NO ANSWER! My heart sank and I went into a panic. I called my aunt whom I always called when my mom didn't answer. I received no answer. Next, I called my grandfather and he said in the most calm voice ever - "Don't worry. Everything is going to be okay." My heart was racing as I continued to try to reach my mom. Still no response. Now, I really didn't know what to do, because MOM always answered; there was never a time she didn't answer for me. Well, I took a deep breath and I continued with my scheduled day. I went to breakfast, and was coming back to my room to get dressed for the activities that had been planned for the day. When I got to my room, I sat on the bed, and said to one of my friends- "something just doesn't feel right." And boy was my gut instinct right! Just then there was a knock at the room door. When I opened the door, I was shocked to see my aunt standing there. In that moment, we fell to the ground hollering and screaming, and all I remember saying is- "where is my mom? Is she alright?" My breathing was out of control; I went into a panic attack. I knew from that moment on, that my mother was no longer here! Real life didn't set in for a long time. I had so many emotions during that time of my life. I remember calling my best friend who literally cried with me all the way from D.C. to North Carolina. and I was speechless, numb, lost, sad, angry; these were all the feelings I felt.

My pain went from angry and sad to pure bitterness; I had lost all faith. I turned to the streets and started hanging out in an attempt to push all the pain away. I didn't care and I most definitely felt God had forgotten about me. I was so bitter because I didn't understand why my mom was gone. I wanted to scream- "Why? I'm just 17; she is going to miss all the important things in my life." But in that moment, God reminded me that He is always with me. He will be a mother to the motherless and a father to the fatherless. I saw people mistreating their parents and not caring, and my heart just tore for them. You only get one mother and father and you better cherish them and the moments you have with them. One song that I used to listen to by Vickie Winans says- *as long as I got king Jesus, I don't need nobody else!!* That song stuck with me for years because I was reminded that all you need is God; He has all the qualities a mother has. God sacrificed his only son. Mothers make sacrifices every day. God heals and children think their *mommy* can heal anything. God makes you feel secure with him just as you feel secure with your mother. The point is God can be everything you need him to be if you allow him.

I can look back over the years and say I'm so glad I made it because there was a point when I felt like I died when my mother died; literally. I remember crying out to God saying- "God, I want to live." At that point, my life was up and down. I didn't know if I was coming or going. I worked and worked to mask the pain until I couldn't any longer. It took years of prayer, therapy, crying, going to church, and now writing it all out, to truly heal. Don't hold pain in, because it will make you bitter and hateful because you have so many WHY questions. You never will really understand, but know God is with you every step of the way! It is okay to not be okay. It is okay to seek therapy, because truly it can help you navigate in ways you may not be able to do on your own, It is okay to take your time grieving, but **don't let the grief consume you** because you don't want to look back and realize the pain is still there and the years have passed but you have got nothing accomplished. I know now that my mom will always be here in spirit, and now I can talk about her and smile, and maybe even cry. However, the tears aren't the painful tears, they are joyful tears in remembrance of the loving woman my mom was and sharing her life with my children so they know how great of a grandmother she would have been to them. Now, when I do things, it's all for my mom and my children. I still want to make her proud. I still want her to see that she raised a wonderful, independent, young woman that still loves God. I'm still standing; I share my story because it could have been different.

I truly am blessed and grateful for the growth over the years. I may have drifted away from church and God, but let me tell you one of my favorite verses that I kept in my mind- Matthew 17:20- *And Jesus said unto them, because of your unbelief: for verily I say unto you, if ye have faith as a grain of mustard seed, ye shall say unto this mountain, remove hence to yonder place; and it shall remove and nothing shall be impossible unto you.* This verse meant so much because I knew as long as I had faith the size of a mustard seed, I knew in my heart God could turn things around for me. Eventually things did turn around, and I thank God for his grace and mercy over my life. Despite losing my mom early in life, God blessed me to have a number of motherly figures in my life. Today I can see that God was with me through it all; back then my grief kept me from seeing His presence. At some point, each one of the mother figures that God placed in my life, supported me when I couldn't support myself. God knew the plan for my life. However, at that moment of loss, I was too lonely, sad and heartbroken to understand. God always reassured me He was right there and never let me go! I thank my village of people that supported me even in my bitter and angry phase. They still loved me and prayed for me. Between my support system and my really seeking and delving into the word of God to get understanding, I was able to heal and see things in a brighter light. My days aren't dark anymore and the pain is now bearable. I chose to live and not die, and I thank God for not letting go of me. One scripture I would always recite is Philippians 4:13- *I can do all things through Christ that strengthens me,* and I mean, I walked with it in my purse every day and when I felt lost, empty or sad, I always go back to the word of God. I knew God was there and I knew mommy was looking down upon me and saying- "that's right baby girl, keep pushing and keep fighting. I'm right here with you!"

Lastly, remember to pray; pray until you see a change happen in your life. God is here and he does listen. We, as people need to sit quietly and listen to that little whisper that guides you every step of the way.

A COMPILATION OF STORIES OF VICTORY

OUR STORIES
His Glory

SPEAKLIFE SERIES

*I press on toward the goal
for the prize of the upward
call of God in Christ Jesus.*

Philippians 3:14

Sean Bethea

Sean Bethea

Lesley "Sean" Bethea is the mother of four adult children and the "Glam-Ma" of seven. Sean's favorite thing in the world is learning. She is obsessed with information. Sean enjoys movies, especially going to the movies, sometimes twice a week. Sean is currently the caretaker of her 90-year old grandfather. She finds great pleasure in serving as his caretaker.

They say if you want to make God laugh, tell him your plans. I guess God thinks Sean is a comedian. Sean hopes that her story will not only uplift you, but give you a renewed faith in God.

There's Beauty in My Brokeness

In June 2016, I had another outpatient surgery on my left knee. See pain and I are very acquainted with each other. I have had arthritis since I was about six years old. I can even recall as a child, being up all hours of the night, beating my legs; trying to get them to stop jumping, jerking and hurting so painfully. My parents were told that I could grow out of it, but we didn't put too much faith into that diagnosis. It continues to amaze me to this day the way doctors think they have all the answers.

I have had over 12 knee surgeries and procedures. I have had metal rods, metal plates, and at least 72 stitches. My legs looked like a Frankenstein experiment! My routines changed. Having another routine arthroscopic procedure was a very normal thing to me, until it wasn't. I woke up the next day with a little pain, soreness and limited mobility. However, there was also something that didn't look right. In my bed, there was a really big wet stain. First thought, did I wet the bed? No, that was too far down for me to have done that. I called my son, JaQuan's girlfriend, Brittany, because my son had gone out of town for work and left Brittany in charge of me until he got back.

Brittany got to my house around 12 pm and we headed to Duke Orthopedic Center to speak with my doctor. When we got there, we found out that my doctor was on vacation. I was met by a young intern, sucking on a Blow Pop. While we were in the lobby, he looked at my knee. As he continued to suck on his Blow Pop, he told me, "Go back home because some drainage was normal. If it continues, give us a call." and he walked away. I felt like he just dismissed me and my leaking knee, but I knew better and proceeded to Wake Med Emergency Department. See, I have had enough of these procedures to know something was seriously wrong.

We arrived at Wake Med at 4:00 pm and my knee was throbbing, and the bandage was soaked from whatever was leaking. I could barely walk and the pain was very intense. They immediately took me to the back and looked at it and told me politely that it looked like I may have an infection, but since they hadn't performed the surgery, I should go back to Duke and they would call ahead to inform them that I was enroute. for me.

With JaQuan on the phone and Brittany right by my side, we arrived at Duke's Emergency Department around 6:15 pm, but unlike Wake Med, they were not so quick to treat me. They took me to a room, but they left me there while my knee continued to throb and leak; and now it's the size of a cantaloupe! I became more irritated by the minute so I decided that I was leaving and going home to elevate and ice it. Brittany is not a talker, not aggressive and surely not bossy, well not towards me. She raised her voice and told me firmly but politely- "You are not going anywhere, sit down, and wait on the doctor to return". I simply cried and cried because at this point, the pain was no longer intense but almost unbearable, and in a matter of minutes, things went from bad to really bad.

The nurse came into the room and said that they would give me something to numb the knee because they had to drain that fluid off. However, when the doctor returned, he stated that they couldn't give me anything as he proceeded to stick a 3-inch needle into my knee. Once the fluid was finally drained from my knee the pain eased, and Brittany and I waited for the staff to return to possibly discharge me, but that did not happen. The doctors returned, but this time, things were moving really quickly. They began to explain that the fluid was a result of an infection, they were going to be taking me into emergency surgery. The next question was- "Is there anyone else that you need to contact?" I began to cry uncontrollably, my heart felt like it was going to jump out my chest, and I noticed that the pain had become excruciating.

The next thing I remember, they were taking me to the operating room and trying to ease some of the fear that was rapidly growing.

I remember waking up seven days later, my son, JaQuan, was the first face I remember seeing. I found out that JaQuan had not left my side and he and Brittany stayed with me every night. JaQuan began to fill me in on what had happened; my prognosis and my diagnosis. It seems that I had been in a coma for a couple of days, then semi-conscious. They had performed surgery five times and as a result, I may not walk correctly for a while. I didn't quite understand what he was saying, but I just thanked God that I was alive! Apparently, my knee had become infected and that infection had spread throughout my entire body in a matter of seven hours; my own blood was killing me by becoming toxic.

I had developed sepsis, which is a life-threatening condition in which the body is fighting a severe infection that has spread via the bloodstream. The condition causes low blood pressure leading to poor circulation and lack of blood perfusion of vital tissues and organs. Medical journals say that patients with sepsis and no ongoing signs of organ failure have about a 15%-30% chance of death, but patients with severe sepsis or septic shock, like I had, have a death rate of about 40%-60%. Of course, I could not comprehend the severity of what had happened to me at that time.

I could not move my left leg, I couldn't walk, I hadn't had solid food in a week and I could not remember any of what had happened. Only during the last week in the hospital did things start to become somewhat clear. I stayed in that hospital, in that same room, in that same bed for 45 days! They even had to go back in before I was discharged to make sure all of the infection was completely gone. The infection was so severe that I had a PICC line in my arm that delivered an antibiotic to me that took one hour and 15 minutes to run.

Finally, it was time for me to leave the hospital, but I didn't go home, I was sent to a rehabilitation center where I was the youngest patient there. I was horrified. I was in a wheelchair, I couldn't walk, I still had that PICC line. The rehabilitation center was gloomy and it smelled like DEATH! I think the Grim Reaper had a room there. I was so scared that first night, the halls were long, dark and so quiet. I kept say "Hello, is there anybody here", over and over. I still couldn't walk but, at this point, I could stand with assistance. Since nobody was answering me, I decided that I was going to call JaQuan and tell him to come and get me. However, that did not go as I planned because the next thing I knew, I was on the floor and the wheelchair was across the room! At that point, I could hear squeaking of wheels coming towards me and I began to cry and the fear that the Grimm Reaper was actually coming to get me took over. I started sliding on the floor trying to out crawl whatever was coming for me. I looked up and it was a resident in his wheelchair looking down at me shaking his head. I kindly asked him if he could please go and get a nurse, orderly... anybody to help me off the floor!

On my official first day there, my son came and we met the staff and discussed the plan for me that included occupational, physical, and mental therapy. I began to adjust and progress very well at the rehabilitation center. My daughter, Crystal, began staying with me, at least once a week, and other family members began to visit on a regular basis. I could come and go as I pleased. I continued to get the antibiotic and they had to keep changing it from arm to arm. I had so many off-site doctor appointments as the weeks just rolled on by. I had to go to a follow- up appointment with a specialist at the Infectious Disease Clinic. There was a concern about how fast the infection had spread throughout my body. When I arrived and saw the specialist, she began asking me routine questions. Then the specialist asked how my son was doing. I just assumed because JaQuan had been there the entire time, the doctor was being nice. Then, she began to tell me that my son had saved my life. She said that on the fourth day when I was at the hospital, the doctors told him that there was nothing else they could do for me. The infection had me. It was on its way to my lungs and I had developed pulmonary edema in my lungs. They couldn't stop the infection and I might not make it through the night.

The specialist then said that my 18-year old son looked at all of the doctors in the room, and said politely, but sternly- "It doesn't matter how many more times you have to open my mother up, you will. See, my mother is a God-fearing woman and He has the final say, not you guys". The specialist then said- "We did exactly what he said, and went back in an additional time and removed all of the infection that still remained."

I went back to the rehabilitation center and I was in such awe of what she had told me. The tears could not stop flowing; tears of joy, tears of enlightenment to know that my God did exactly what He said He would do. Knowing that my son, who had been in church all his life, who knew that my faith was in God, stood firm on the word of God and because of that I am a living witness today! I stayed in that center for 45 more days before I was released to go home in a wheelchair. I had outpatient physical therapy. I went from the wheelchair to a walker, to crutches, to a cane, then to walking unassisted; all in the matter of a year.

The doctors also said that I would never walk right again. That was in 2016. In 2018, I *wobbled* all over the dance floor at a family function! And in 2019, I was running around for my high school class reunion! Nothing can stop me now!

I believe that 2016 was the year that God chose as one of my testimonial years because in May, I fell backwards down 15 stairs. While at the emergency room, they gave me a CAT scan and discovered that I had apparently had a mini-stroke within the past couple of weeks. On June 1st, my oldest daughter, Chantall, gave birth to my first grand-daughter, Faith Love, at 26 weeks. I had the honor of being there when she came into this world weighing only 1 pound. For the next four months, I was constantly praying for. Chantall and Faith, since I could only see them through pictures. I prayed for Crystal and JaQuan because they were running back and forth trying to take care of everybody. I prayed for my son Jerry because he was out of town and couldn't be with us, and mostly I prayed, for myself. See by this time more fear, doubt, sadness, and even depression had begun to weigh heavily on my mind and in my heart. Now, along with my broken body, my mind and my spirit was becoming broken too. I couldn't be there for my children or my grandchild, like I had always been there for them. The hits just kept on coming and on October 16th, which is my son Jerry's birthday, his fiancé' gave birth to twins at 37 weeks. Faith had been in the Neonatal-ICU for the past four month and now, so were the twins, Nasir and Nevaeh. I now had three grandchildren, all in the NICU at the time, together in the same room. I was walking short distances with one crutch and was able to visit my grand babies. On November 21st, I turned 46 years old and on that same morning, after only being home with her mother for a short time, my granddaughter, Faith Love, gained her Heavenly Wings. She was only five months old.

In 2016, I learned not to take anything or anybody for granted. My FAITH was tested, twisted, and surely broken, but because of the God I serve, He never left me and never did he forsake me.

Today I still deal with mental and physical pain. I take a lot of medicines, and I sometimes have a slight limp, but by His grace and mercy, I am still here!

There is so much beauty in my brokenness!

Sharon Dye

Sharon Dye

Sharon Dye is a Special Education Consultant with over 17 years of experience working with children and families in the state of Michigan. She's a native Detroiter, mother, grandmother, Surge 365 travel club member and Team Builder, a blossoming speaker and author, founding member of The Real Business Team Detroit and CEO and Visionary of Sunshine Bridges. Sharon received both her B.A and M.A degrees from Wayne State University in the areas of Human Developmental Psychology and Teaching. Sharon Dye has provided her services within school districts, through online group forums, and through independent consulting. As a result, she has directly impacted children around the world. Her educational background in Human Developmental Psychology and her expertise in providing special education services for children and their families has given her a broad base from which to approach many relevant topics and concerns. Sharon is a survivor and overcomer and shares her story with women who are experiencing challenges in their lives. When she's not inspiring young scholars to excel in school, she enjoys spending her time mentoring girls and women, going to Zumba, and trying out new recipes in the kitchen with her granddaughter Aniyla.

You can connect with Sharon at:
riseandshine365@gmail.com- (313) 748-3481
For FREE online Tutoring Services and Coaching in Basic Reading and Reading Fluency,
visit: www.sunshinebridges.com
For Home Based business opportunities visit me at: surge365.com/riseandshine
FREE and Unlimited usage of my Discount Travel Site at:
www.myvortex365.com/riseandshine
Booking Packages of Travel: ytbtravel.com/riseandshine
Follow her on Facebook and Instagram at:
facebook.com/theaudacitytoshine/?modal=admin_todo_tour
facebook.com/sharon.dye.73 & instagram.com/sharonevetted/

From Surviving to Thriving

I t was years before I recognized my life had true value to the world. I sensed there was more to my life than my early experiences. I remember, often feeling unsure, unsafe and unbalanced. The foundation at home felt unstable and shaky. I know I wasn't in control, but no child should have to grow up worrying about *everything*. Today I know with certainty, God was always by my side. My experiences were never meant to hurt me, but to mold me for the woman I would become one day. God wanted to use my life as a testimony and a *survival kit* for someone else. My challenge was figuring out how to align with a God I didn't know, in a world that didn't always accept me.

I used to think God was an inaccessible spirit in the sky. I had no true relationship with Him and didn't truly understand how He worked in my life. When I was little, whenever God came up in conversations, it was as if He was either passing out blessings or punishing someone. During Christmas and Easter, He was mentioned more, but still there was no relationship built with God; it was just attending church twice per year. I suppose you could say my family upheld a different set of morals and values.

Growing up, I didn't feel as worthy as the other girls around me. Because of this, I began unconsciously *watering* myself down for the approval of others; which I rarely received. I spent a lot of time alone: in pain, shame, doubt and confusion. In my heart, I knew I was different and that I would be okay if I could just survive my childhood years in one piece. Somehow, I was aware that I was going to have to work harder than others to just be *normal*. I didn't know much about prayer during those days other than, "Now I lay me down to sleep…". You're probably wondering at this point, "what happened to her to make her feel that way and not know God?

My story began during the Christmas of 1973. My daddy passed when I was three years old. I believe the events surrounding that experience caused the foundation for early trauma in my life. I have always been told that I was a *daddy's girl*. One of the *secrets* was that my dad wanted a daughter, and my mother didn't want any additional children by him. It was whispered that he took his *husbandly rights* from her one night and that *forced union* produced me. When he passed away, my mother slipped into an impenetrable emotional coma, leaving me alone: lost, and confused. I wonder if she was trying to figure out what to do with this girl who looks just like the man she wasn't in love with.

I know now it wasn't all her fault, because she was born into a family heavily yoked in secrecy, and unforgiveness: entangled in generations of strongholds. My mother grew up watching things being swept under the rug, and she learned to not question anything. My grandma had multiple children by multiple men whom she never married or built stable relationships with. She instilled in my mom and her siblings that it didn't matter who their dad was, if they knew who their mom was. I know this led to shame, guilt and resentment in so many ways because some siblings grew up knowing and interacting with their dad, while other siblings never knew their dad. I believe my mom inherited emotional instability from the generation before her. Their world was raw, and this left my mom unable, unstable and unequipped to truly know how to fully love, embrace and nurture her own children.

As a result of this, I was often passed along to my aunt. It was almost as if I was subliminally being taught what my mother thought: that "once *he* was gone there really wasn't a use for this girl I never asked for." I am actually very grateful to my mother; she realized that in her heart, she didn't fully have all that I needed. Although I lived in the home with her, and my brothers, she felt her younger sister and her husband would be better equipped to give me the *something* that she couldn't. I spent a lot of time with my aunt and uncle growing up, and never really understood why. It wouldn't be until later in my life that I found out my dad had pre-arranged that set- up before he passed away, knowing he was dying. It is said, my dad didn't trust leaving me alone with my mom, in fear of her inability to *love his baby*.

We lived in a small home on the eastside of Detroit. I have three brothers and I am a middle child, including all the implications which come along with that title. I didn't receive a lot of attention growing up, I didn't receive much instruction growing up, and I didn't receive much love growing up. What I did receive was a roof over my head, a minimum of one full meal per day, a pair of shoes, basic clothes, and whatever else came along with survival. There were extended times when the heat, lights and water were turned off and kerosene heaters, electric heaters, candles, and buckets of water were used to survive. You become very creative and crafty when you grow up in survival mode, because you learn things that most never experience or can relate to. Things like cleaning and drying your clothes in the sink and hanging them near an air vent when the gas and water were on. Heating water on top of a kerosene heater or a hot plate to use to wash up. Hanging up a sheet in a doorway when there are no doors. Finding privacy in a two-bedroom home when you have three brothers sharing a bedroom with you. There were times there wasn't much to eat other than frozen meats in the freezer, which my brothers and I had no idea how to prepare as young children. My mom worked daily from 7am to 3pm and during summers and school breaks. We were left at home by ourselves. This began when we were eight, seven, five, and one years old. One summer, my oldest brother set the house on fire and we almost died. Some family members and people in the community rumored that my mom and my baby brother's dad tried to do it for insurance money. The lies that people tell! However, that is what happens when we leave ourselves exposed. We all know how people talk. However, those days were very dark and dismal for me. I was so unhappy and depressed. I wanted to feel loved and safe, but I just didn't feel that way. I guess my mom was looking for her own love during those days opposed to an *assigned* love. I say *assigned* love because my grandma, the survivalist, had chosen my dad, an older man, for my mom.

I will never know if that was her truth or not because my mother passed away in 2017, along with her secrets and pain. I thank God that before she passed, she tried her best to make amends with me. She gave me my childhood home and said that Charles, my dad, would have wanted me to have it. In later years, she finally began hugging me, and occasionally gave me an awkward kiss on the cheek. She loved both of my sons unconditionally and gave them the love and adoration she was unable to give me. Towards the end, she began telling me that she was proud of me, respected me as a woman, and would even seek my counsel for moral dilemmas she trusted my judgment with. She never actually said the words- "I'm sorry. I love you Sharon" before she passed away. Maybe those words had been too painful for her to say all those years before. Yet, now I know that the words were her truth. I was sorry that my mother had been unable to express her love to me during the years I needed it most.

Throughout the years, those experiences left me with ISSUES: mommy, daddy, emotional, rejection, abandonment, and anxiety. For many years, those issues made it difficult for me to create real bonds with people. It led me to choosing an abusive man for a husband, allowing myself to be used in multiple fruitless relationships, opened the door for hurting others, and delayed some of the blessings God was attempting to send into my life.

After a while, I learned how to cut men and women off *with quickness*. It was easier to look for flaws and sabotage any inkling of a relationship with someone who was attempting to invade my space. My truth was, I was afraid people would see how broken I truly was. A lot of people gravitated towards me, but I was ill-equipped to handle their high expectations. After all, I was trying to be invisible: yet, appear normal. I had enough to contend with at home, and adding demanding friendships to my life was not part of my survival plan. This led to me hurting and abandoning many people who simply wanted to get to know Sharon. Then there were others who couldn't relate to my vibe. They would call me fake or weird, leading me to sink further within myself. Instead of arguing with them, I would just retreat and let them believe things that were not always aligned with my truth. These experiences taught me very early on, to stay away from people as much as I could and only deal with them when I had to. I remember being little, and silently declaring that- "I wish people would just leave me alone!" There was a kind of peace in my solitude and loneliness. I was different like that: it was my preference. My family just wrote me off as being very shy. I wasn't shy: I was anxious and uneasy around them. I was only my true self around a couple of people in my little world. I couldn't trust just anyone to do right: I was compelled to protect my sensitive and fragile self. I figured that I was better off figuring this life out on my own. I felt that I just needed a few good people to enter my life and help me figure out how to be *normal* like everyone else. I figured if I could just get people to *like* me I could make it to adulthood.

Those survival mechanisms led to the beginning of searching for love and understanding in all the wrong places. As I got older, life seemed to become more difficult. Being different led to more rejection and isolation. I learned that fighting and avoidance were two necessary tools for my survival. I was always in fight or flight mode. I lived most of my early years surviving off pure adrenaline. Can you imagine how exhausting that was? While others were learning to thrive and develop self-confidence, I was trying to just survive another day.

I knew my life was different from the other kids at school, and in my neighborhood. I used to daydream about being a kid who was safe and free to just be. My fight wasn't always a physical battle, most of the time I was fighting against internal battles within my mind. I mainly wondered what it felt like to have a mom who told you that- "you are awesome and can accomplish great things." I wondered what it felt like to have large family gatherings with strong men and happy wives around. Mostly, I wondered why everyday had to be a struggle. I couldn't really relate to females because a female, *my mother* was the first person to reject me. I couldn't relate to the males either because I was very shy, a late bloomer and the males around me didn't make me feel safe and secure when I was in their presence. Not to mention, growing up in the city, you had to have the latest styles and hairstyles. Most probably have no idea that growing up in Detroit during the 80's and 90's meant you were a nobody if your clothes, family, and hair didn't make you a *somebody*. Go back and read that last sentence again. Ultimately, this led to me dropping out of high school and having my oldest son just so I could get on public assistance and get my life started *by myself.*

I know that sounds terrible and I certainly wouldn't recommend that level of logic to anyone ever! Many people have *someone* they can go to. However, many others have *no one* and make extreme decisions to survive. Don't worry because that was my *then* and this is my *now*. I went to college and obtained both a bachelor's degree and a master's degree, became an educator, author, speaker, and business owner. God is currently using me to guide, educate and mentor our youth and I am more than happy to accept the assignment. After all, I know some tactics that can help someone navigate around the roadblocks of life when no one at home is responsive. Life is funny like that. It starts off one way and can move a totally different way depending on the choices we make.

God never intended to give me a life of pain, but the world gets a hold of us sometimes, and causes damage to our life plan. That damage can be used to either catapult our lives into a living breathing testimony or a sad and pitiful story. The choice is always our own, because we have free will. I know God can do exceedingly and abundantly above all I can ever hope for or imagine in my life. But there was a time when I had no idea about that and felt so alone. I am thankful that He never left me, even when I didn't know how to love myself. God's spirit in me always had the softest and meekest voice. It was that voice which got me through my darkest times.

I didn't always trust or know the real me, due to a deeply internal negative self- image that stayed with me for years, because of the way my life started off. If I couldn't trust myself, then how could I trust that soft voice within me? This was why I began turning to other broken people for guidance. I wasn't wrong for desiring guidance in some form or fashion. My downfall was that I looked to people who didn't have a relationship with God, and were not the best counsel. After all, how can the blind truly lead the blind? Often those influences have led to me partaking in some very broken relationships. What's funny is those people abandoned me, misunderstood me, distracted me, talked about me and everything else they could do when God began moving in my life. *But God* strategically removed, replaced and realigned my circle of influence with *His people*. He can do it for you too, I promise!

I learned so many lessons along the way *from surviving to thriving* and placing my life in God's hands instead of in the hands of people. I now rely on God's power, because He alone is able. The voices of the past always try to get in my head and say- "who do you think you are?" or "you're not qualified". Now I know that I can speak to those negative thoughts. I can say- "Get thee behind me Satan. I am a new creature in Christ, and I can do ALL things because He said so! My Life Has Value!!!

A COMPILATION OF STORIES OF VICTORY

OUR STORIES
His Glory

SPEAKLIFE SERIES

Satisfaction lies in the effort,
not in the attainment,
full effort is full victory.
It is better to conquer yourself
than to win a thousand battles.
Then the victory is yours.

Tonya Miller Cross

Tonya Miller Cross

Tonya Cross is the owner of Accented Glory and The Vine Event Planning. Accented Glory is a handcrafted women's fashion accessory brand that specializes in natural hair accessories and afrocentric jewelry designs. The Vine Events is an organization that hosts informative events, such as personal development and small business workshops. Cross merges her two passions to share with fellow creatives, ways to gain online brand visibility. Cross' designs have been featured on Essence.com and MarthaStewart.com. Tonya has been married for twenty-seven years to her high school sweetheart and has three beautiful daughters. Cross' first book anthology embraces the opportunity to share her spiritual journey. Her hope is that readers learn from her experiences and pick up the knowledge gems dropped in this anthology. To learn more visit accentedglory.com and thevineevents.com.

Choose Life

Self-Love

Have you ever wondered what self-love really means? Well, it goes beyond pampering yourself with a spa day. Best believe, there's nothing wrong with a great massage or mani-pedi. I happily indulge in these activities myself and love every minute of it; however, self-love is much deeper than an occasional trip to the spa. Self-love is defined as a regard for one's well-being and happiness.1 I know for some, this statement may sound selfish. Trust me, it is not. For a woman that once lacked love for myself, self-love is necessary for my preservation. My start in loving myself began with forgiveness.

I'm a woman who grew up without my father in the home. I never knew why my dad didn't come around much, and his absence impacted the way I saw myself. I questioned if something was wrong with me and blamed myself for him not being present. My self-love journey gave me the courage to stop carrying a burden that didn't belong to me. I learned that other people's decisions and choices, such as my father choosing not to be active in my life, were not a reflection of me or my worth. I had to release myself from not feeling good enough and overcome it with positive affirmations.

My earliest childhood memory is of me walking on a dirt path lined by tall grass with my mother and brother. This path wrapped around the back of our neighbor's white cement block house across from our home on a dirt road. I remember us all carrying our own brown paper bag that held the necessities my mother decided we needed for our walk to her parents' home. I don't remember what was in my bag, but I do recall fearing what we left behind and what lie ahead. Unknowing to me at the time, that paper bag contained more than the earthly possessions of a three-year-old-- it also contained abandonment and unworthiness. All of which created baggage that I carried for many years throughout my childhood, and well into adulthood. This baggage eventually began to impact my choices and self-esteem.

Five years after graduating from college, I worked for the Guilford County Health Department and my husband and I had purchased our first home. My husband, Michael worked for Polo Ralph Lauren, and we had three young daughters, Deseré, Cierra, and Gabrielle. From the outside looking in, life appeared to be fabulous. However, inside I still felt empty. I had fallen into a routine that lacked meaningful purpose and impact. I felt something was missing that went beyond material things. One day during my quiet time, I read a scripture that resonated with me in that moment. The words in John 10:10 leaped off the page and into the heart of that three-year-old girl still inside of me. It promised me a life of abundance that I was currently not experiencing.

The words of the scripture were so captivating that I couldn't stop thinking about it, so I decided to take a deep dive into God's word in hopes of gaining a better understanding. This decision started me on a new journey towards self-love. Unlike the dirt path I traveled with my mother and brother when I was three years old, my new path was a pathway to forgiveness, healing, and restoration.

My Story

My parents divorced when I was four years old. I didn't fully understand the impact of not growing up with my father until I reached adulthood. I learned that as infants, our guardians' ability to respond to our needs shapes our expectations. Repeatedly unmet needs throughout childhood can negatively impact our adult relationships. Our family dynamics can also impact how we engage with others. A child's social behaviors are often a reflection of what they see and experience at home. During my childhood and teen years, I longed for my father's love and presence and those unmet needs led to feelings of abandonment and unworthiness.

My father reached out to me my sophomore year in college. I was attending UNC-Chapel Hill, pursuing a pharmacy degree. He wanted to reconcile our relationship. I agreed to do so with hopes of getting answers. I wanted to know his reasons for not coming around often. For a few months we talked on a regular basis, and sometimes he would drive to Chapel Hill to visit me at school. In a very short period of time, we began forming the bond that I had always wanted as a child. During that time, I learned a lot about him and how much we were alike. From similar mannerisms and world views to both having a love for learning, I was surprised to find how much we had in common! Then I got a call only months into our new relationship; informing me that my father had died from complications of diabetes. The news was so devastating that I don't even remember who it was that called to inform me that my father had passed away. That day my life became a blur and I lived in a fog for the next few years. I also never got my answer to why he never came around much; once again I felt abandoned.

The year following my father's death, I was accepted into pharmacy school. During my second year in the three-year program I became pregnant with my first daughter. I chose to keep my baby because I felt obligated to my unborn child; I knew first-hand what abandonment felt like. I didn't want to become my father. My high school sweetheart was my daughter's father. He was attending North Carolina A&T State University and was able to make most of my doctor appointments. After our daughter was born, I made the tough decision to leave her in my mother's care while I returned to school to complete my degree. After graduation, I got a pharmacist job working at Revco (CVS) and eloped with my longtime boyfriend; we were married at the Greensboro Courthouse.

Although I've never witnessed a marriage relationship up close and in person, marriage was something I desired. I loved my boyfriend and daughter and wanted them to have a relationship that I didn't get to experience. The early years of our marriage was tough because of unresolved childhood issues and we found ourselves needing marriage counseling. During a counseling session, I realized that I was imposing my *daddy issues* on my husband. I had an underlying fear of my husband leaving our marriage; abandoning me and our children just like my father did my mother. This fear led to unwarranted mistrust in my husband. Looking back, I thank God for blessing me with a husband who truly honored our vows when we promised to love each other for better or worse!

Marriage counseling also revealed that I held myself responsible for my father's absence. I questioned what was wrong with me. Was there something about me that kept him from coming around? Believing that a personal flaw was the reason for my father's absence fueled my need to excel. I felt the need to be the best at everything I did. In my mind being the best would make me a desirable daughter; someone of whom a father would be proud. I became an overachiever. Yet, my father still did not come around. I excelled academically and set high goals to accomplish to numb my pain. This type of life by no means was living abundantly. I was carrying the burden of not having a father; I thought it was my fault he was not around, but that burden did not belong to me. My father's choice was not a reflection of who I was or was not. He made the choice not to be actively involved for reasons I do not know. I had to learn that it wasn't my place to decide whether his decision or reasons were valid; that was his cross to bear not mine.

His Glory

"The thief comes only to steal and kill and destroy. I came that they may have life and have it abundantly." (John 10:10 ESV) I took a personal deep dive into John 10:10, a dive that lasted for years because I desired a full understanding of what an abundant life looked like. I wanted to identify the thief in my life and be aware of his need to cause harm. On the other hand, I also needed to figure out how to embrace and live an abundant life. To my surprise, the principle of stewardship was the key to it all.

My deep dive into the verse, exposed that I was the thief. I was the one robbing myself of joy. I had to come to terms with the fact that sometimes we can be our own worst enemy. I had allowed my father's choices to influence my perception of myself. Our mind is a battlefield and renewing it is a daily task. To renew means to return to a former state. As humans made in the likeness of God's image, our original state is innately *spiritual.* One of my favorite quotes by Pierre Teilhard de Chardin is "We are not human beings having a spiritual experience. We are spiritual beings having a human experience." As spirit beings, we should also be spiritually minded, allowing our thoughts and actions to be influenced by the Holy Spirit. We have to remind ourselves that we are more than our struggles and that we possess value and worth. I've come to learn that life more abundantly is life that goes beyond mere existence; it's richer and fuller with purpose and meaning.

When most people hear the word stewardship, they instantly think of money, but it's so much more than that. By definition, stewardship is the proper management of another's property. The bible gives us a perfect illustration of a good steward in the Parable of Talents. (Matthew 25:14-30). In the parable I learned that being a good steward positions you for more opportunities. How well you manage what you already possess will determine if you have what it takes for more. There are two relationships that form the foundation of stewardship: God/Man and Man/Man.

God and Man

God is the creator and owner of all things and man is the manager of these things. God's original plan was for us to have authority over things we possessed. (Genesis 1:26-28, 31) Unfortunately, because of the disobedience of Adam and Eve, the script flipped; instead of man having dominion over things, things now had dominion over man. (Genesis 2:15-17; 3:1-6) My false beliefs about my value and worth had control over me. Blessings can become hindrances when we use things without regard to God's intentions and instructions for ourselves. I misused my relationship with my husband to try to fix something broken in me. Thank God for His Son Jesus! His coming restored God's original plan for us. The principal of stewardship exposed how I was mishandling my marriage and how to take authority over the negative thoughts of myself.

Man and Man

God values relationships and we're accountable to God for how we manage our relationships with others, including ourselves. In order to have successful relationships with others, we must first learn to love ourselves. One of my favorite songs is "Bag Lady" by Erykah Badu. Two verses in the lyrics speaks life to me, "All you must hold on to is you...I betcha love can make it better." As we go through life, we pick up bags (baggage). For me it was abandonment, unworthiness, and unforgiveness. I was a bag lady dragging many bags; creating a form of self-bondage. The bondage gets in our way and hinders us from walking in God's promises. We miss out on what God has for us because we're unwilling to let go of our bags. We also bring the baggage into our existing and new relationships, making it difficult to truly love and be loved.

My struggle with abandonment and unworthiness has taught me how to be a better steward of my relationship with myself. When you love yourself, you see yourself as God sees you. Yes, it's true we all have faults and issues, but God sees beyond them. I had to stop allowing my thoughts and what I believed to be thoughts of others to rob me of experiencing an abundant life. To effectively love others, I had to first love myself. In learning to love myself, I was also able to forgive myself. I forgave myself for not seeing my own worth or value. For not embracing the fact that I'm made in the image and likeness of God and possess the authority to pull down and overcome strongholds. In addition to forgiving myself I had to forgive my father. The resentment I held towards him, even after his death, blocked me from experiencing all that God desired for me.

Victory in my struggle also lead to me becoming a better manager of my relationship with others. I stopped carrying burdens that didn't belong to me. I learned to take control of how I respond to and interact with those with whom I have a rapport. Like self-love, this is an ongoing process! I started by becoming opened to being loved without fear of being hurt or disappointed. My new mindset has greatly improved my relationship with my husband and others.

Choose Life

In every situation we're faced with two choices: life and death (Deuteronomy 30:19). When we choose life, we choose to believe and value God's truth. You may ask, if it's truly this simple; why do I have such a difficult time making the right choice? Unfortunately, our beliefs and values were established before we committed to God. Our beliefs and values are learned through our experiences, environments, and educations. Because of this, it's an ongoing process of unlearning false beliefs and values. Practice makes perfect and eventually it'll become second nature! Renewing my mind activates the principle of stewardship in my life. More opportunities come my way because I understand that I have earned and deserve a spot at the tables I sit at and have built.

Today I want to encourage you to choose life! My self-love journey led me to a life of abundance and I desire the same for you. Because of God's word, I was able to overcome my struggle with low self-esteem. My feelings of abandonment and unworthiness were a direct reflection of my relationship with my father. However, the principal of stewardship taught me how to love myself and others unconditionally. I learned how to affirm my worth and value daily and embrace an abundant life. Are you ready to experience abundance? Then start examining your relationship with God, yourself and others. ***Choose Life!***

A COMPILATION OF STORIES OF VICTORY

OUR STORIES
His Glory

SPEAKLIFE SERIES

*A prayerful woman knows where
her victory comes from.
That is why, she stays on her
knees, no matter the season.*

Gugu Mona

Toy Jones-Jackson

Toy Jones-Jackson

Toy Nicole Jones-Jackson is a Durham, North Carolina native, widow and mother of two college-aged daughters. Toy is a certified licensed travel agent and has had a business in this industry for the last four years. Toy is also employed with the United States Government Veterans Administration, where she has worked for the last fourteen years. She enjoys serving those that have fought for our country, including her father, grandfather, and uncle. Toy considers her job to be the best way to honor them.

Our Story His Glory is Toy's first book project, as a co-author. In her chapter, *Rejected for Purpose,* Toy gives you the realness and rawness of her story, sharing the beginning of her journey. Toy's chapter is filled with broken pieces, terrible choices, and ugly truths. It will also expose every reader to her major comeback, how she found peace in her soul and a love. Toy's story exposes readers to love on another level; not just your ordinary love, but an unconditional love with no limits. This love molds and shapes Toy into the mother, widower, friend, sister, daughter, and author that she is today. This love saved Toy's life.

Rejected for Purpose

My rejection started out at an early age, before I even knew who I was or how to even capture my own identify. As I grew older, my eyes opened to what I was facing and I was able to identify that rejection was what I was experiencing. While rejection was eating away at me, I covered it up. I knew how to put a band-aid over it. I suppressed my hurt and feelings. I moved through life, as if I was okay; always appearing strong to many. I was covered in band-aids full of pain.

While I was dealing with my own pain, I compensated by identifying the rejection in others. It was like a gift. Hurt people seemed to gravitate to me. Immediately, I wanted to fix them, help them, build them up. It made me feel good and somehow I felt I was healing myself, only to find out I was not.

I can remember, being in the 5th grade. It was one sunny morning in May. I got up full of happiness and joy, extremely excited about my graduation. As I got ready that morning, I found a white dress with ruffles at the bottom of my closet. It wasn't new, but it was my favorite. I adored that dress and thought it was just the most beautiful dress in the world. I got dressed and did my hair and got ready to leave for school. Before going, I asked my mother if she would be coming to my graduation today. My mother was also getting herself ready for work. She replied that she would not be able to get off work early to come. I responded, "ok" and headed off to school. I wore my dress all day until it was time for my 5th grade graduation ceremony. While I was excited to graduate, the only memory that stuck out from my ceremony was looking out to the audience, at all the families, friends, and parents and not seeing my own. After graduation, the parents ran to the children hugging them, bringing flowers, and balloons. As I watched in envy, still smiling, I hugged some of my classmates and said, "See you later".

I started my walk home in my white ruffled dress and ponytail, held together by a flower bow. I walked in my white sandal flip flops. As I started walking down the long two-lane road home, I remembered families passing by blowing and looking. I looked up and waved at them and put my head back down. One particular classmate stopped. Her dad asked me if I needed a ride home, I said no. They asked me if I was sure. I said I was and smiled and continued walking. They drove off. Even through my smile, thoughts flooded my head, but I was really too young to understand totally what I was feeling. I felt embarrassed, but I quickly brushed it off. As a coping mechanism, my childhood mind started to take over and I made that lonely walk home from graduation an adventurous fun one. I walked home singing, skipping, and talking to myself on a two lane road, that I'm sure most would have said was too dangerous for a young child to be walking. As I reflect back, I wasn't walking alone, God was walking right beside me.

As the years passed, I entered my pre-teen years and faced rejection and loss in an even greater scale, as my best friend, my big brother, was temporarily taken away from me. My Big Brother was four years older than me and absolutely the best big brother. He always protected me, looked after me, and never allowed anyone to harm me or disrespect me on any level. We had that normal big brother, little sister bond. I would always go hide under his bed and listen while he talked to his girlfriends. He would always find me snickering and pull me out from under the bed and thump my head. It was true sibling banter. My brother wanted to be a DJ and I can remember that I used to love to watch him play his music and mix his turntables. He really loved it and had a lot of passion for it. We both share a lot of the same characteristics. We both carried a lot of heart and love, even if it wasn't reciprocated, we still showed love. That's just who we were.

At the age of 17, my brother got into a little trouble and was sent to a Juvenile Detention Center for 10 months. It felt like three years to me! I missed him dearly and the feelings of rejection came flooding back. I had to find a way to deal with it. So, once again, I let my imagination take over. I blocked the pain and hurt of missing my big brother, by putting a band-aid on it. Who would I tell my secrets? Who could I trust? Who would protect me? Even though I was and remain a "Daddy's Girl", its nothing like having a big brother. I depended on him, I needed him. This time of separation was the start of my trust issues. I completely lost my inner voice.

In middle school I remember being teased, a lot because of my dark skin. I was never the girl that got invited to the slumber parties or birthday parties by her classmates. I began to believe I was those names I was being called and I started acting out. In middle school, I was known as a trouble-maker. I always got caught doing something wrong. Somethings I didn't even do it, but I was assumed to be guilty. When I tried to defend myself and speak up, I was blamed anyway! All they would have to say is "Nikki Jones did it," and no one believed me. I started believing that I was that bad person that others said I was. When I felt isolated and defeated, I would always run to my imagination to cope. It was my safe place.

I allowed people to tell me who they thought I was, and because I did, I lost my confidence. I couldn't speak up for myself, so again, I put another band-aid on my hurt and pain. I quickly became a people-pleaser. I wanted friends and I wanted people to like me, so I started being the class clown. My goal was to make people laugh, whatever it took. I would clown and make my classmates laugh, thinking that would make them like me. I would lie or dress things up to make it look good for me, all in the hopes of attracting friends. I would get invited to things, but that didn't really work the way I intended. Instead, I was just known as crazy "Nikki Jones".

While I felt labeled and rejected at school, back at home, in the neighborhood where I grew up, The West End, I had real friends. My friends there really understood and connected with me. (We are actually still friends to this day.) I'd rather be in West End than out in the country, which is where we lived. I did a lot of mischievous things because I hated being in our new neighborhood. This was my parents' first time purchasing a house. As I look back on it, I know now they were only trying to do what they thought was best for their family, but again, I hated it there. Any opportunity I had to get to the West End, that's exactly where I would be.

My parents had a lot on their plate keeping a home together. They both had two jobs each as I can remember. My mom worked full time at the local clinic pharmacy. After work, she would go to church for practice, she was the church pianist. Mom had to be at church for everything: choir rehearsal, bible study, anything that required her to play, she had to be there. She was also a den mother for the boy scouts. Mom did a lot. She put a lot of time in at work and at church. My dad was always working as well. By the time that we got home, during the week, he was there and sometimes he would have dinner already made for us. Sometimes we went out to eat, because my mom wouldn't be done with church duties until late. Study time, homework, things like that were never enforced. Most of the time, I did it on my own time. My Dad would help me at times, if I had a question or needed help, but nothing was ever structured. Really important things like the "Birds and the Bees" conversations, as the old folks would say, were never really talked about.

I remember when I started my menstrual cycle. When it happened, I knew what it was and was excited and nervous. I remember my dad going out buying me some sanitary napkins. I think we called my mom and she told me what to do and how to use them and that was that. I faced my high school days as a still shy, timid and insecure youth. I was still a virgin, while nobody that I associated with was. Of course, even though I was still a virgin, I had to play the part as if I wasn't. Only my best friends knew the truth, but to be honest, I was terrified to even have sex. I really knew nothing about it, only what I heard. It hurts the first time. You can get pregnant on your first time. Through all of this, I still had that wild and adventurous imagination. I was a risk-taker. I would try things that others would not, but wanted to. Those were things others admired in me, but never told me.

As the high school years rolled by, I would catch some of the cruel words directed at me, but not as much as in the past. I was able to find some confidence in things. Having my true friends around me helped a lot, but deep down inside, I still felt like that little girl walking down that two lane road home from 5th grade graduation. I still felt like that teenager in middle school who was scolded for any and everything. I still believed deep down that I was all those things people called me. REJECTION consumed me. By this time, the band-aids were all over me. The pain and hurt was buried, but very much still alive. I became someone I was not.

As time passed, I met a guy through a friend. Now, I knew nothing about holding a mature conversation with a guy and I'm pretty sure he picked up on that quickly! He could quickly sense my vulnerability and used it to his advantage. This relationship started the absolute worse six years of my life. At times, I still cry, thinking of how I was treated; abused mentally, verbally and physically. The only good thing that came out of that six-year experience was towards the end of it, I received the greatest blessing ever my first born, my daughter Khayah. At twenty-one years old, I gave birth to my first born. When she entered the world, it was love at first sight. It was an "unconditional love. When I looked at Khayah, all I knew was that when she grew up, REJECTION would not be part of her story.

Towards the end of this six-year experience, towards the end of it, I dipped and dabbed with other guys, nothing serious. This was before Khayah was born. There was one guy, who I knew when I was a little girl, but as he said in a joking way, "You are not that lil chocolate girl standing in your grandma's fence and can't come out anymore." We laughed and I said, "nope, sure not". We connected a little here and there, but nothing serious (at least I didn't think so). He had plenty of women, definitely a ladies' man, but somehow when we were together, he made me feel really special. Even though we weren't serious at that time, there was a connection. You know that feeling you get when you want to leave a person alone and forget about them, but you really can't because they always pull you back in. It was always "FIRE" when we got together.

Shortly after that, I became pregnant. Though I wished my firstborn was by this special guy, I knew deep down that she was not. I had to tell him. Shortly after I shared my daughter's paternity, we drifted apart but still had that special connection when we saw each other around. After Khayah was born, she gave me the push I needed. I was slowly finding my inner voice again. She saved my life and gave me the strength to walk away from the abuse and manipulation in my existing relationship that I had endured for the last six years. After ending the relationship, I felt a huge weight lifted; I wasn't being controlled or used by this person anymore. My confidence was stronger. I was a mother, someone depended on me. I was going to make sure I never failed her.

A year and half later, Khayah was about 18 months old, and word on the streets was that my old fling, that special guy, had served some jail time and was back home. I put the word out to tell him that I said, "what's up". Maybe a week or so later, my special guy showed up at my front door. "I heard you've been asking about me," he said. Looking back on that very day, I would have never thought that I would spend the next twenty-one years with this person. Two years later, we created Aaliyah, my second born. I became a woman because of this person. Soulmates is what we were. Our love was rare and you don't find that type of love often. The band aids were off. Love healed me; not your ordinary love, but an unconditional love. For me and my daughters, this love healed my brokenness.

My rejection was for a purpose, it pushed me to know real love; unconditional love. The love that was needed in my life. I could walk into my purpose now. The walls were down and the band aids were off. Love conquered all. True Love, Real Love never ends. Our story begins here. Thank you **Arthur Allen Jackson**. Continue to rest peacefully, the love of my life.

Umeka Jackson

Umeka Jackson

Umeka Jackson is a native of Detroit, Michigan. She currently resides in North Carolina, with her two daughters. For over twenty years, Umeka worked professionally as a Real Estate Legal Professional. Umeka is truly multi-faceted with passions in fashion, self-care, culinary arts, interior design, event planning and travel. Umeka combined her passions to start *PAMPERING STYLES*, a mobile spa business, providing a variety of self-care services and products.

Umeka is a woman of faith, who has faced many adversities in life. As a wife of over sixteen years who recently became a widow, Umeka felt pulled to tell her story of the importance of the marriage vows that we take. Umeka wants everyone whose ever lost a loved one to know that you don't have to grieve what you've lost, but cherish what was shared.

How To Live Through The Vows We Take:
Til Death Do Us Part

I t is our wedding day; the very day we dreamed of celebrating our love with our family and friends. We planned the perfect event, from the decor, music, food and the very small details to create the ambiance to make sure that day is everything we dreamed of, and goes exactly the way we planned.

But we often downplay the most important part of the day; the vows we take. They are not cliché; the vows are designed to shape our lives for our marriage, throughout our years together. As we pick out the rings to symbolize never- ending love, we must also pick the symbolic marriage chain to make sure it is unbreakable and capable of holding the husband and wife together. The weight of life is not meant for one person to carry.

We like to be selective and pick the most favorable parts of the marriage vows. We love- *to have and to hold. For better or for worse,* we always want better and never want to face the worse. *For richer or for poorer,* we only want riches and forbid the lack thereof. *In sickness and in health,* we never want to face sickness more than the common cold, and we take health for granted *til death do us part.* We recite this vow, but what do we do when we have to live it out?

EACH VOW WE TAKE IS A LINK IN THE CHAIN; THEY ALL MUST CONNECT TO CARRY US THROUGH OUR MARRIAGE

Nothing lasts for a lifetime, but our marriage should be the best time of our life. Not to say, we won't have opposition, and there will be some tough times. However, we vowed to face it all together; we knew the trials would come with time. No matter how long the marriage may last, we will have to live through what we vowed; so what do we do?

TO HAVE AND TO HOLD

It is the first vow we recite; due to its tie to when we first fell in love. We were delighted to have somebody to adore us, protect us, to love us, and to have our back. That is where it begins. We accept our spouse as a gift from God. We imagine holding on to that *forever feeling*: it is the beauty of love for one another. What will we do now that we have it? How long are we willing to hold on to it no matter what?

FOR BETTER OR WORSE

As we are in love, life will happen, things will not always go according to plan. Life will be interrupted. As we recite this vow we are saying that we are willing to stand together in the good times and the bad times, with the one we love. We know we will have successes as well as times of defeat. Yet, together we will stand, hand in hand, no matter what.

FOR RICHER OR FOR POORER

We recite this vow to stand together, to value each other in any capacity; we can fall individually but we can stand stronger together. Many marriages start out with two people at the beginning of their careers. They may not have much when they start, except for their dreams, goals, plans and their love. If they also have faith in God and put Him first, then they have an excellent start. The key is to seek God's guidance as they work together as a couple to work their economic plan. Even with the best laid plan, the value of the dollar depreciates and money comes and goes; but the couple must always value the love that they share. If they maintain a three-strand connection: God-Husband-Wife, they will always be prepared for what may come.

SICKNESS AND IN HEALTH

We recite this vow to stand together no matter what physical, mental or emotional ailments may befall us as a married couple. Love means caring enough for each other to support each other in making healthy decisions. We have to be present and be accountable for each other whether we are healthy or experience a short-term illness or a chronic illness. This vow can be demanding. However, we vowed to not abandon our marriage partner due to the uncertain hardships in life. We promised by our vow, to love through it all; to show always that our love is true and can withstand the test of time.

TO LOVE AND TO CHERISH

We recite this vow, realizing that in a marriage there will be good days and bad days, successes and defeats, life triumphs and life trials. We vow to always hold on and get through all aspects of marriage by loving and cherishing each other. The Bible tells us that- *a man will leave his father and mother and be united to his wife, and the two will become one flesh. (Ephesians 5: 31-NIV)* With a connection of this magnitude, the couple should demonstrate love, respect, and fidelity towards each other. They are one; they should operate in unison. With no regrets knowing that you did it together.

TIL DEATH DO US PART

Because we never know when it will be our last moment together, we must value our partners and our commitment to the vow that we share. ***TIL DEATH DO US PART.*** We recite this vow, promising to stand together against everything the world will throw at us. We will DUCK, STAND, CRY, LAUGH, SUCCEED, FAIL, GROW, LOVE until death do us part. As we connect the links of our life moments together, we can face this vow and live on; Love on.

Vows are the links in the chain of marriage. It's beyond the perfect wedding day that we dreamed of. As we dream of that perfect day, we must think beyond the wedding day. Together, as husband and wife, we must carry the chain, pull on it, and make sure there are no weak links in our union chain; never letting it go. Our chain should be unbreakable. When the chain is strong, that's when you know you are ready to make that perfect day you dreamed of, your reality and cultivate a successful marriage.

I was willing to carry the chain until I had to lay it down. Suddenly, without warning, living our lives like we had for the past sixteen years; life changed forever. Our marriage chain was broken by the loss of my partner.

A Dedication to Renaldo Mario Jackson (Buff):
We said "I Do" and we did, til death do us part. I still smile, every day, as the morning star rises and shines on me, letting me know you are at peace. I never imagined that the worst thing I could ever imagine enduring, could bring me so much peace. The alternative could have been devastating, but **God Makes No Mistakes, My Love.** *No matter what happened, we never let go of the chain. My Friend, My Husband, My Angel,* **FOREVER**

FOREVER

Don't get stuck at the grave, don't grieve what you lost, but always cherish what you shared. Knowing you once loved and you can love again; every day and every moment matters. Don't take having your spouse's presence, their touch, and the talks for granted. It can all slip away, in the blink of an eye. Daily, you must cherish your "Forever" on this earth. From the best days that you share, to the worst days, the happy times to the sad times, the laughter to the tears, the health and the sickness- do not take your love for granted. Link every moment together and always cherish what you have as a married couple.

Throughout your life, make sure you secure and strengthen your marriage chain. When you are forced to live through the vow, *Til Death Do Us Part*, remember that your chain still remains unbreakable. The vows of a marriage are also how we have to approach both life and death. We must cherish every moment and understand that every life decision causes an action and reaction. Some good and some bad. Just as in a marriage, we are connected to others by God's design and purpose. It's up to us to shape the marriage chain so that it can withstand what is promised in the vow; for we must live and we must die.

What you do together, during marriage, prepares you for facing the departure of your spouse; *Til Death Do Us Part.* You will grieve because your spouse will be missed, but you will cherish what the two of you had, your unity chain. Always remember the memories you made. When you have to face that ultimate vow, due to come, you can smile because HIS will was done.

SPEAKLIFE SERIES

laticia@laticianicole.com
Tel: (919) 407-8528

LATICIANICOLE.COM

OUR STORIES
His Glory

SPEAKLIFE SERIES

A COMPILATION OF
STORIES OF VICTORY

THANK YOU FOR YOUR SUPPORT.

Made in the USA
Columbia, SC
09 June 2020